Into
ers

For the turn-of-the-century BAMBACE sisters

Angela, February 14, 1898

Marie, March 28, 1899

ALIVE FOREVER

INTO THE LIVES OF OTHERS

MOMENTS OF CONNECTION

Athena C-H Warren

The Tiresias Press, New York City

Library of Congress
Catalog Card Number: 94-060555
International Standard
Book Number: 0-913292-03-6

Printed in U.S.A.

Published by
The Tiresias Press, Inc.
116 Pinehurst Ave.
New York, NY 10033

Royalties designated for
Second Mile, Inc., Williamsburg, MA 01096

COVER BY PAUL CHEDA

CONTENTS

Foreword, *by Bet MacArthur* 7

Beginnings 13

First Year 19

Second Year 65

Third Year 95

Fourth Year 121

Endings. 151

Epilogue, *by Ruth Carson West* 153

Acknowledgments 157

FOREWORD

There are those who will talk for an hour
without telling you why they have
   come. And I? This is no madrigal—
no medieval gradual.
   It is a grateful tale—
without that radiance which poets
are supposed to have—
   unofficial, unprofessional. But still one need not fail

   to wish poetry well
   where intellect is habitual—
glad that the Muses have a home and swans—
that legend can be factual;
   happy that Art, admired in general
   is always actually personal.

— Marianne Moore*

The most personal art is made, when it can be made, by
people who possess nothing else—people young or old whose
words, gestures, rhythms, or melodies are all they have to
contribute to the world. Displacement, oppression, violence,
disease—any of these can threaten a person's world and everything she or he has: roles, relations, material possessions, the
mirror of community, the mirrors of the self. In orienting to
loss of many kinds, play, exploration, and expression become
the bridges from old identity to new roles.

Even in the midst of deprivation, the self can be discovered.

* "In the Public Garden" © 1959 by Marianne Moore, from THE COMPLETE
POEMS OF MARIANNE MOORE by Marianne Moore. Used by permission of
Viking Penguin, a division of Penguin Books USA Inc.

Simple acts of human connection, or the briefest tentative curiosity about form, color, or sound can ignite this discovery. When the place can be made safe enough to risk changing the uses of a single moment, the living self can be awakened, no matter how long it has been shielded. Often, the energy and permission for experimentation first have to come from outside the self—from someone daring to gaze back, offering a mirror for the waking face, welcoming expression.

Athena Warren has such energy, and also determination and curiosity, and with these she gives the most sublime invitation and permission to others. As the text that follows will reveal, she created an opportunity to do this in an unlikely place—a nursing home in Western Massachusetts—and, in this diary of her four years' work there, she has fashioned a tale which is destined to become a classic account of re-awakening personalities, a valuable guidebook for relational practices of many kinds.

If, among the ordinary environments of American social life, there is one where people most routinely expect to be left with virtually nothing, then surely the nursing home is that one. The very words "nursing home" provoke a response—euphemisms are used to name "that place." Our expectations of possibility there are limited, usually. Among all the ordinary institutions of American life—our schools, churches, hospitals, even our prisons—the nursing home has come most to represent the dreads we all share: dread of disability, isolation, and neglect.

It is a paradox that nursing homes were originally conceived to provide a way for the ill and disabled to be "out of hospital," "in the community," and "closer to home"—yet instead, nursing-home placement has come to mean being "out of family," "displaced," "out of community." (That each nursing home itself becomes a community, with a practical rhythm as well as symbolic systems all its own, is often overlooked. Residents, regarded from outside as a cast of strangers, quickly form relations for themselves in a closed environment.) So, while nursing homes exist in practically every community in our nation, rural as well as urban, from outside their walls they remain nearly invisible. Their stigma affects the way everyone associated with the home is perceived—staff (defensive or dedicated), family members and friends (helpless, uncaring, or hopeful), and residents (disabled, lonely, brave). Surely this paradox affects you, the reader, as you enter this story with whatever doubt, curiosity, or hope you bring.

Make no mistake about it—the social invisibility of nursing-home residents is traced to the stigma of disability. Some of this fear is displaced upon the elderly, as people persist in associating the nursing home simply with old age. In reality, it is disability or illness, not only old age, that brings residents to a nursing home.

But exactly how does it happen that the nursing-home resident is displaced, devalued, seemingly left with nothing? Especially if the facility is well-run, nursing care is good, staff are competent and even dedicated, and even in cases where the resident has reason to look forward to discharge and greater independence some day? The answer lies not in the quality of medical care, nor in the provision of pleasant surroundings, but in the way we form our social world.

To become disabled or ill, to enter a nursing home, is to lose one's established social roles. Along with whatever adjustment to illness or disability, or perhaps to facing the ending stages of life, the resident must also adjust to a *new social role*—the role of being a *patient only,* the role of *no-role*—most particularly, a role in which little is expected for the resident, and even less *of* the resident. This process of *role loss,* and its relation to disability, is explained by sociologist Erving Goffman in his landmark text of 1963, *Stigma: Notes on the Management of Spoiled Identity.* Not only for nursing-home residents, but for disabled people everywhere, the impact of such lowered expectations can be oppressive and destructive. Throughout our society, the vulnerability of disability and difference operates as a social distraction, somehow disqualifying individuals from their own familiar social roles (as parent, worker, homeowner, consumer, citizen). When these roles are presumptively erased—not by the physical demands of living with a disability, but through our behavior with one another—diminished expectations change the shape of our social world. When others expect little of one, few opportunities are presented in which one is asked to give to others. As less and less is expected, one learns to expect less and less of oneself. Thus, to accept the role of nursing-home resident, disabled and out-of-community, gradually one must learn to forget oneself.

Athena Warren's diary reflects this reality in a particular way, because it begins with her approach to the residents through simple art media. This method of working with disabled and institutionalized people is well-established, and rightly so, particularly because, in regard to the social construction of disability, it has a special meaning.

Involvement with art media rehabilitates individuals socially as well as physically, because the imagining, planning, and execution of even the simplest design involves communication. Along with the physical gratification of working with materials comes first the experience of frustration during learning, and finally the satisfaction of resolution—an artifact, a product, however incomplete. But our social construction of the role of the person producing this product also is always operating, shaping the meaning that we assign to the results. That creative work by a disabled person might be about anything *other than* disability and loss confuses us. That a creative impulse and expression would emerge from a person's *essential self,* and not from the part of the self defined by a disability, is difficult for others to perceive. And if one's disability is neurocognitive, affecting one's mood, thinking, memory, or speech, then expectations are even lower—even more persistently may others assume that there is no longer room or energy for creative discovery, nor for the impulse to give, to play, to share with others.

Athena Warren decided to bring creative-arts activities and friendly visiting to the residents of a modern nursing home. She studied and understood the role of "safe play" in the process of leading disabled people back toward claiming their essential identities. Starting out using art media, she stimulated people to explore, express, and make connections with their inner selves, with one another, and with their memory of the past.

What directed Warren to do this work, it seems, is her extraordinary drive for relational contact; and her absolute conviction, born of experience, that there was virtually no one she could not reach. In her notes she reveals herself to be a master of discernment, sketching in the heart of each new person an ever-expanding map of possibility, reflected in the mirror of relationship. Of her goals, she wrote, "I wanted all the infirm to become alive and be pleased with themselves. I wanted old-sick and old-healthy people to know that they could still experience varieties of freedom." With each resident, no matter how long out of communication, no matter how limited by disability or discouragement, Athena Warren had the drive to welcome, to reach out, really to reach *in,* to the lives and spirits of disabled women and men—without hesitation, judgment, or fear.

Into the Lives of Others is not, after all, a text about disabled artists, but about the lives of institutionalized and forgotten people. Neither is it a furtive critique of what is wrong or what is right about the institution of American nursing homes. Athena Warren's diary is a study of what is gained by searching for connection, for the essential spirit in everyone. It is a guidebook to the process of fostering communication and relationship using any medium at hand—whether art materials, gardening, household objects, or even the mundane treasures in the bottom of a lady's handbag.

Into the Lives of Others is an account of the process of mirroring the functional parts of the self, using any means available to return a sense of that self to the one who has lost it. Warren enthusiastically and unconditionally greets any degree of opening with the warmest welcome—and any degree of shielding with the warmest respect.

Finally, what is most compelling about the diary that follows is that it was written unself-consciously, without premeditation. It was not conceived as an account for posterity, but only as a means for the writer to track her observations, justify her interventions,and communicate to a handful of staff about her encounters with residents whom they knew. After the diary was closed, and Athena Warren's four years at the nursing home were ended, the immediacy and aliveness of its story took on a new value. As a found narrative, *Into the Lives of Others* transcends the particular lives of its characters to reveal an enduring message about the foundations of human connections, and our never-ending potential for healing and growth.

—Bet MacArthur, MSW
Cambridge, Massachusetts

BEGINNINGS

At fifty-six, I dreamed up a career for myself.

From the Yellow Pages of a telephone directory I picked a nursing home at random, phoned the administrator, and asked her if she could use another person on her staff to work with residents. What I could offer were interpersonal skills and creative-arts techniques.

"Come tomorrow," she said. "Any time. We'll talk."

At the interview I told the administrator about the graduate work I had just completed in a program called Planning for Play (a program affiliated with the Massachusetts Department of Mental Health and the University of Massachusetts), and I went on to describe the nursing-home ambitions that I held dear.

I wanted to "unfasten" the imagination of patients.

I wanted to make a connection with any given patient through conversation.

I wanted to convince old-sick and old-healthy people that they could still experience with pleasure, even if only to a small degree, some of their five senses: seeing, hearing, smelling, tasting, and touching.

I wanted to bring to nursing-home work (on however small a scale, in whatever way possible) the concept that play, movement, and communication could be experienced by incapacitated people of any age.

I described to the administrator how my ideas about what I could do in a nursing home came about in the months of field work in the Planning for Play program. First, at the Belchertown State School, I and my fellow students observed children with a wide range of disabilities and learned how to create (or otherwise acquire) suitable play facilities for them. For example, we designed a padded tray that enabled a hydrocephalic child to hold up her head. Later, some of us worked at a local nursing home that had a children's ward attached to a large wing for 120 adults. There, together with several of the nurses and several of the maintenance staff people, we built an experimental outdoor play area, with results that went far beyond all our expectations. Special intergenerational areas were designed for different kinds of motion and activity. Patients were wheeled down a ramp from the main building to specific function-areas, and almost immediately there was significant evidence of their interest and involvement.

Imagine a severely arthritic woman doing "exercise" motions holding a crayon, and then, when asked to draw something she loved, making random stabs at a sheet of paper and producing a drawing that was meaningful to her. "This was my dog," she said.

Imagine little people with fragile and distorted bodies throwing themselves fearlessly onto the rolling surface of a new waterbed and feeling the joy of physical emancipation.

Imagine dormant and beautiful feelings awakened in old people as they tentatively caressed those little bodies.

Imagine courage, affection, and hope . . .

[And then, with a sigh, the administrator said, "Of course, we could not do any of that here." I shrugged my shoulders as if to say, "Who knows?"]

I knew long before I was graduated from that superb and exciting Planning for Play program that I wanted to continue this work with old people. Perhaps it was my awareness of the limited survival time of nursing-home patients that drew me to them. Surely that must have been part of the explanation for my wanting to work with old people—*they were running out of time.*

At my nursing-home interview, I said that I was certain I could help out in both the activities and social services departments. In neither department would I be intruding—I would only be supplementing their work. I felt that individual attention was needed to regenerate in patients the desire to live. I would have the energy to do just that.

Evidently I had arrived at this 40-bed rural nursing home at the right moment, for I was hired. They labeled me "a facilitator." They said the kind of work I would do was up to me and the residents. Any two days of work per week were offered me. I chose Thursday and Saturday, the latter being that part of the weekend when activities and social services were ordinarily not on hand and therefore the day could be expected to be dull.

I was asked to keep a journal about my contacts with the residents. The journal or "Communication Book" as the staff members sometimes called it, was left in the office, always available. Thus, the staff maintained a connection with me and my work, and I was also able to note my progress, promises, and mistakes. Here and there a colleague entered a comment. By the end of my fourth year at the home, the journal contained over 400 (5½ x 8½) handwritten pages. As it was written, it is presented here, edited only for clarity.

Into the Lives of Others is not a book of case histories. Nor is anything in it confidential. It is a record of institutionalized old people's efforts to reach out to me, a middle-aged stranger; my efforts to reach into their lives; and their occasional efforts to reach out to their fellow-residents. Connections were made—spiritual, intellectual, emotional.

The journal starts with five women:

COLETTE, heavy and crotchety and in a wheelchair. Noisy.

LORRAINE, slender, amiable, and quiet. Needing no help to walk.

ELIZABETH, impenetrable, almost a sphinx in a wheelchair.

MARY, considerably younger than the others, observing everything like a bird as she masterfully wheels herself in and around.

MARGARET, deaf and very old, with lots of affectionate family. She joins the group some days later, walking slowly on her own.

In order to establish a relationship, we started working with clay. It would take time to loosen imagination. Art objects could be realistic or not. I wanted to see self-initiated work that spoke for the person creating it. I wanted residents to make something without feeling controlled; without there needing to be something accomplished; without the work being judged right or wrong, or pretty or not pretty.

Later on, with other residents, different techniques for establishing rapport were used like introducing my little granddaughter Rebekah to a resident named Pietro, and their going for a walk hand-in-hand; like inducing Ron, another resident, to start a vegetable garden with me.

Always, I wanted to see a nursing-home resident begin to make a connection with another person. My aim was to lessen feelings of isolation and help rekindle in residents an ability to connect with others.

That old people could be lured out of their institutional lethargy, I never for a moment stopped believing. I was just as sure, as my work progressed (and as I view it today), that many more ways than I had thought of could be found to enable family, volunteers, friends, and staff to make contact with any given resident.

As the journal proceeds, men and women drop in and out. Some we lose track of. I, too, am sorry.

I offer this journal as a testimony to the joy of stepping into the constrained lives of others and helping to make a diference.

The torch is lighted.
I pass it on to you.

Opening a diary for the first time is like walking into a room full of strangers. The reader is advised to enjoy the company without trying to remember every name.

— *A Midwife's Tale* *

*By Laurel Thatcher Ulrich (1990). New York: Alfred A. Knopf, p. 35.

FIRST YEAR

Thursday, May 27

Colette, Lorraine, Elizabeth, and Mary all participated in their first "Art Experience." This is what Esther, the activities director, called it.

Yesterday I was presented to several patients in the sun room as a person with whom they would have fun, so today we started with modeling clay, warming one small blob at a time, rolling it into a ball. Colette in a wheelchair, mumbling in a French accent, sat near the side wall. I brought over a place mat and a large spoonful of clay and placed it all on her lap. Colette rolled the clay into a small ball as instructed, but within minutes she handed it back to me. She said she preferred to do some *real* work with her hands, like sewing.

Lorraine sat silently at the table with me and made a beautiful small ball, set in a clay saucer of her own design.

Esther introduced Elizabeth. She was pulled up to the table with Lorraine and me. Elizabeth is severely arthritic. She thought that her fingers very likely would not be able to make a ball, but she was able to make many very small balls and thought she could squeeze them together.

Colette wheeled around, rejoining us off and on, just observing.

Mary, rather younger than everybody else, was wheeled into the room. She sat at a distance, close to the entrance to the room, and asked to stop there. Esther handed her a blob of clay. Mary worked silently, warming and rolling the blob around.

When I first arrived in the building yesterday morning and

was introduced to Mary, I expressed an interest in her needlework. I asked her if I could bring my own lap-size oriental rug with me when I came next time so that she could help me mend it. She does beautiful needlework. Besides, I like getting a patient to be the teacher, reversing the roles.

At the end of our session today, all the clay was returned to a plastic bag. Lorraine hesitated to return hers until she felt that she had removed "all the wrinkles" from the clay. Then she handed her ball and saucer to me. In a soft voice she casually expressed interest in folk tales and myths, noting that my name was Athena. We talked about Athena the goddess, and I promised to bring in a book on mythology.

I said goodbye with a handshake to everyone in the sun room, not just those four working with me but some 16 or so people, mostly women. Sometimes I shook the dead hand, sometimes the other hand. Most everybody has had strokes and I find it is important to acknowledge the stroke, which I do by literally referring to the hand as "dead." It never fails to bring a response of relief from the patient. It's like calling a spade a spade. I know there are those who are squeamish about being so blunt. To me, exaggeration is better than pussy-footing. There is something offensive about one's affliction not being understood as being as serious as it is.

It will be a problem to decide how much attention to give to which people. Do I wait for them to seek me out? I don't think so. Perhaps the activities director can help me judge.

Saturday, May 29
[Note from social worker]
Athena, Dropped in for a few minutes this morning. So glad

you're here.   —*Louise*

Lorraine was resting in her room but was easily persuaded to walk down to the sun room to work with clay. She made a small bowl with very little assistance from me. At the end of the session I walked her to her room and left her holding the oversize mythology book which she had agreed to my bringing in.

Mary reminded me that I had said I would bring her my oriental rug. She worked with clay for a bit, making what looked like a simple trivet, and then was eager to get to her needlework, which was back in her room.

Colette joined us with no hesitation. She made a bowl but did not think it looked like one until she decorated it with blobs of clay, which might be fun when it comes to glazing.

We used real clay today; the modeling clay will not be used any more. It is too difficult.

I found that working with three people was comfortable for us all. That just might be the optimum number. Nobody else was even in the sun room today.

Thursday, June 3

Lorraine made a human face out of her clay and asked to keep it. She described it as a tired face and then, after adding ears, she described it as an elephant. She said the head made her laugh.

This is Mary's third experience with clay and I do believe she rejects the challenge of extracting something of personal interest from a hunk of clay. She flattens every ball into a plate. The challenge is for me to discover what is meaningful to her.

Margaret (one of Mary's roommates), a newcomer to the group, worked with her blob of clay without asking for instruction. She smiled as she pulled into existence a head, two arms, and two legs. She was very pleased with her creation. When we walked back to her room, she asked to have the clay figure placed on her dresser.

Everybody seemed to enjoy the hour, as did I. I already felt a connection with Mary, Margaret, and Lorraine. No sign of Elizabeth and Colette.

Saturday, June 5

This time we worked in Mary and Margaret's room, just Mary, Margaret, and I. It was comfortable and there were no distractions. We sat down at a table.

Margaret, who is quite deaf, was splendid. She was totally engrossed. She again made a person and added it to the other one on the top of her dresser.

Mary, flattening clay on the table, used the opportunity to comment about people in the institution, what their schedules were, and where they would be going during the week. And all the while she was slapping away at the clay.

Lorraine was resting in her room down the hall and did not want to join us when I went to invite her. Sorry not to reach Lorraine, although I spent some minutes with her after the art session. She seemed so removed that I put my arm around her and she expressed pleasure in the contact. Colette also preferred to remain in her room. Elizabeth was reading.

Thursday, June 10

During the first half hour (again in Margaret and Mary's room) we worked with clay: Mary, Margaret, and Lorraine. Each of us made a medallion with a hole, and we put them all to dry on Margaret's dresser. At some point these objects will be collected and brought to a kiln. We also made small beads each with a hole so they can be threaded into necklaces.

When Lorraine belittles herself, I laugh at her need for perfection. Once Lorraine shrewdly grasped the situation and exclaimed that she was succeeding at failing. We laughed together, and she and I smiled at the connection we were making with each other.

For the next half hour we worked with shaving cream. We made landscapes with shaving cream, each on our own plastic mat. We worked our fingers into the cream, making mountain peaks. Then we made paths on that terrain. This was done by my saying, "Let's take our fingers for a walk." Immediately, Lorraine said she was lost. So with *her* finger we retraced the path back to where she had started and once more set out. At one point she wanted to take a detour because her sister was on a peak some distance from the path, and then she said, "Let's leave her there."

Never did any of us think we were crazy. We all knew we were making believe. We agreed that not only children make believe, but so do grown-ups. I feel very strongly the importance of playing "make-believe." It is a vehicle for expressing repressed thoughts, a harmless way of getting something off your chest.

Lorraine cleaned her soapy place mat in the sink. We called it a landslide. Lorraine took my arm and we sauntered back to her room. We picked up momentum after she commented on our pace being "like a funeral."

Saturday, June 12

Margaret was dressing herself when I entered her room and she threw up her hands in a jovial but silent greeting.

Another successful day. At least for Mary and Margaret. We

made more beads that will be fired, glazed, and then fired again. Mary was very talkative about her illnesses and her displeasure with her present doctor.

Lorraine was in the sun room. She was agitated, talking nervously to another patient. She took my hand and we went into Mary's room where Lorraine calmed down enough to stay with us for some 40 minutes. Like the others, she made beads of clay, punching a hole in each bead with a long reed. When she expressed weariness (or perhaps anxiety), I encouraged her to go for a walk and then come back to us. She did not return.

Thursday, June 17

Am still waiting to see the results of firing our clay work. If the ceramic pieces survive the kiln, we will glaze them. In the meantime, today we worked in two media: pastel chalk and shaving cream.

Mary wanted to drop out. "Too dirty," was her comment about the chalk. So I gave her a mound of shaving cream with which to design, asking her to spread out her hand on the place mat. I traced her hand with cream and even put a band of cream across her hand, telling her she was "trapped." She laughed.

I constantly emphasize that we are playing make-believe so as not to go counter to their experience in Reality Orientation with Esther and to cooperate with the existing program.

I turned to Margaret and asked her to scribble with the pastel chalk. She did a meticulous scribble of concentric lines.

I did a scribble and then filled in the enclosed areas. Nobody followed me.

Lorraine walked her chalk in random directions and insisted on being lost. I told her that that was possible, but not *just* for her because, in a sense, we are all lost. Our heads, in this game, do not know where we are going. Just our hands know. And so she ploddingly took tiny steps with her pastel chalk and started out in the direction of my finger, which pointed at an arbitrary spot on the paper. She finally arrived there in triumph. I cheered, loud enough so that even Margaret heard. Then Lorraine connected four corners (arbitrarily set down by me), making a rectangle—except that it had a curve in it. I suggested that a baby grand with its own peculiar curve would fit right into that place in the box. Again we agreed that it was make-believe. I asked her to put music in that box and she put down a few notes. I printed (right-side up for her but upside down for me) a few words of the song that we both said we heard coming from the piano in the box. We laughed at our "Coming Through the Rye."

Mary was satisfied playing with the shaving cream and seemed pleased with the feeling of cleaning herself.

Margaret seemed even more cheerful and smiling than usual. She is bright and cooperative.

Saturday, June 19

I invited Margaret and Lorraine, one on each side of me, to go outside for a walk. Mary did not want to be wheeled and remained behind. Margaret and Lorraine and I were outdoors for no more than five minutes when it started to rain ever so softly. Lorraine's only qualifying remark about staying outdoors was, "As long as I don't melt." She has a whimsical sense of humor.

We walked around the building and I bent down to scoop up a small handful of soil. I commented that it was cool. Lorraine responded that her mother would love that soil. And so we talked briefly about mothers. I told them how my mother used to be a good gardener, too.

As we were walking back into the building, Margaret said, "What are we going to do today?" I spoke into her ear and asked her if she had any suggestions. No. Did she want to use pastel chalk again? Yes.

Lorraine, too, was willing to continue to use pastel chalk, but she said she had no idea what to do with it. When we were seated at a table, I asked her to shut her eyes while I made dots and dashes on her paper, using a heavy hand and actually sounding the writing. I asked her to open her eyes and tell me if what she actually saw was what she had imagined she would see. She did, and smiled.

I closed my eyes then and she did a series of dots which I did not hear. Lorraine has a very light touch. What was I trying to do? Make her aware of the visual quality of hearing, just another aspect of the versatility of the senses. But she had fooled me. She had not even drawn dots or dashes. She had taken off on her own and drawn a "fuzzy caterpillar." She described to me how a caterpillar moves by pulling itself up and then stretching, and she drew a second caterpillar doing just that.

I feel that Lorraine enjoyed herself more than usual. She told me she was looking forward to Thursday.

Mary, sitting in her wheelchair, was both interested and not interested. She thought we were crazy, and she really did not want to get her hands dirty. Still, in a sense she actually did get them dirty. She did not scribble but she smeared the chalk, making beautiful shades of orange and blue—strange for not wanting to get her hands dirty. I told her that if that pattern and those colors were on a piece of silk it would be spectacular and would make a striking piece of material for a dress. Lorraine agreed.

As for Margaret, she asked no questions but drew, very quickly, meticulous repetitive designs.

It was a great session.

Thursday, June 24

Some success, but it remains to be seen how much. I thought that Mary, who regularly wants to do nothing, might start making her own designs for needlework. Considerable resistance. However, she did take verbal directions from me, like, "make a square," then "draw a circle within the square." And then "make a circle within that circle," and so forth. She followed directions willingly, but colored the spaces unwillingly. She said it was like kindergarten.

So we accepted that and called the paper "Make-Believe Kindergarten," again making my point that "make believe" is acceptable and necessary to get ideas across.

I hope that Mary will be willing to try doing a design for her needlework, especially since no judgment would be passed on whether it is good or bad.

Margaret, on the other hand, effortlessly drew a series of pictures representing her happy weekend with her son.

Lorraine refused to write her name with the hand she usually writes with, but was willing to use her left hand to write her name. Why?

Then, with that same left hand she wrote the word "HAPPY," and said she could not read it and did not know what she had written.

Lorraine stayed with us a half hour, after which she got up to walk around. She did not come back. I sought her out at the end of my day to say goodbye. I'm sure it matters to her to have me not just drift off, but to formally end the day. What it carries, I think, is the promise that we'll see each other again, in spite of whatever got into her head not to return.

Saturday, June 26

I was greeted outdoors by Mary sitting in her wheelchair, and by Margaret, who was also seated. Lorraine was on a path walking towards me, coming from the small patio in front of the building. I said to Lorraine, "Do you remember me?" She did not answer directly but said she was my friend and that she was expecting me.

I gave Mary my small oriental rug. We need to figure out a stitch to mend it, and she accepted the task eagerly, although she said that she had never done anything like it before. I said I never had either so she would then be able to teach me. I loved being able to switch our roles.

With Margaret I had a conversation about her daughter-in-law whom she is expecting tomorrow. She started to draw a picture of her family, and while she was drawing I went for a walk on the grounds with Lorraine. We discussed her son. She did not remember his name, and she berated herself for not remembering. She said he was smart enough to remain a bachelor.

We returned to the front of the building to see Mary still at work on my rug. I hope I can apply what she teaches me. Margaret was waiting to show off what she was doing. She had started a second drawing, copying her ring. It is a hinge-ring that opens to reveal a tiny picture of her dead husband.

Lorraine did not want to sit with the others outdoors. I offered to read to her, so we went to her room to borrow her roommate's book of poems. Then we went outside again and sat apart from the others and read "Teanor, the Druggist," in which the poet observes how people are similar to chemical elements: people who are okay in themselves may be no good when combined; and the disaster of some combinations, as in some chemical combinations. Lorraine found this poem appropriate, and made the comparison to herself and her husband. This was a breakthrough in our connection, her talking so freely about her husband.

I find Lorraine alert, intelligent, and friendly. I think she works at being helpless, and since I joke with her on the subject, she is becoming noticeably less so.

My purpose with everybody is to establish contact on a personal level, to stir memories of significance, to liven their lives.

Thursday, July 1

Elizabeth joined us today. Margaret and Elizabeth were the active participants. We drew with pastel chalk again. Margaret on her own. She took the initiative in making a design out of intersecting lines. She eagerly used different colors to systematically fill in and decorate enclosed areas.

Elizabeth selected two kinds of weather to illustrate: one sunny, the other foggy. She didn't say why we had not seen her for a month, but it did seem to me that her sunny and foggy bands of color represented her moods. I did not suggest this to her.

Saturday, July 3

It happened! It felt like a miracle. Elizabeth and I were drawing in pencil when she asked me to draw a floor plan of my living room. I drew a plan of my living room and put a baby grand piano in it. Somehow the shape got squinched and I apologized, saying, "That's funny. That looks like shorthand." She immediately said, "I know shorthand." I said I knew Pitman and she said she knew Gregg. Then she told me that she constantly sees shorthand words in random designs. The way children lying in bed look up at the ceiling and see scary faces in a stained ceiling. She said she was once proficient in shorthand.

So we combined our efforts. She wrote "geranium" in shorthand and I drew a design of a stylized flower around the shorthand word. It was fun. And I'm sure we can get a great deal across to each other by this teamwork. But most important was the discovery of a latent skill.

Thursday, July 8
Well, today was good. Worked with Elizabeth and Margaret. We used Elizabeth's shorthand to label a drawing of mine. Margaret was fascinated by the shorthand "scribbling."

I have begun to write notes to Margaret who is so very deaf, and then I don't have to shout.

Margaret chose to draw a "house for sale." Elizabeth, who says she herself does not know how to draw, did express an opinion about Margaret's drawing. "Where is the door?" And then, to me, "Would you put a roof on that way? Wouldn't you connect it?"

So, even though Elizabeth does not draw, she demonstrated to herself that she can see and that she can analyze.

Elizabeth's assignment for next Thursday is to imagine the drawing of a house and how she will direct her hand to put down what she sees.

I told Elizabeth that the reason I would not have a session with her until next Thursday was that on this coming Saturday I want to get back to Mary who is feeling irritable, neglected, and, I dare say, angry.

Saturday, July 10

Elizabeth sought me out. She loaned me a book to read for us to discuss some other time. I'm not sure I'll be able to get to it as soon as she would like. Next Thursday she will draw a house. Mary and I talked about Elizabeth's favorite author, Joseph Lincoln, and Mary could not see the satisfaction derived from reading. Her pleasure is needlework. I would like to see her do an original design. But I must go slowly, lest she think I am knocking her skill.

Thursday, July 15

Elizabeth drew the house of her childhood, indicating her bedroom and all the furniture. It was a composite of an elevation and a floor plan. Very clear to both of us.

She asked me to draw a picture of my present home. I did a conventional architectural floor plan, which interested her. She sees now that she does not have to be an artist to use symbols in a drawing to tell someone something. It is communication.

I think drawing is easier for Elizabeth than working with clay. Her arthritic fingers can manage to hold and direct a pencil whereas pulling and pushing clay take a different kind of strength.

Mary went for a walker-walk with a nurse. She was cranky and tired and did not want to work with me.

Margaret was asleep, which was fine because I then visited Clara, a woman across the hall. I said I would help find a sloping surface for her to play bingo on while lying back in her chair. She misses being able to play the game. And then we might do some drawing on this same board if she cared to.

I agreed with Colette, to her surprise, that she need not do a single drawing for me since she simply does not want to; says she does not know how to and does not want to do what she is "no good at doing." So as a result, we did hit on something for us to do together. She was crying and complaining about not seeing enough of her children. I said I would teach her how to write with her left hand. Colette is willing to start learning by printing the alphabet. One day we will write to her daughter.

The head nurse smiled when she saw Colette sitting outdoors with me. I told her of my hope that Colette would learn to write with her left hand and thus be able to derive satisfaction from writing letters, and pleasure in receiving the answers. The nurse was enthusiastic about providing Colette with this hope.

Have been spreading myself out a little too much, but I think it is inevitable. I cannot drop Mary or Margaret even if I am not actively working with them. So I pick up our threads by stopping to converse with them both and in that way I'm able to maintain my connection.

I did not see Lorraine today.

Saturday, July 17

I greeted some of my friends—Margaret, Mary, Colette, Elizabeth, and Lorraine. Told them that I would be off to Rutland, Vermont, tomorrow for a workshop in art therapy.

Thursday, July 29

Was gone for a week.

Well, it's nice to be back. Lorraine seems a little distant. Things are falling into place. I'll be working for some months with Colette and Elizabeth on Thursdays and with Mary and

Margaret on Saturdays. There is a theme that connects Elizabeth and Colette: each has lost the use of her dominant (right)
hand.

Colette would like to learn to write with her left hand. She is
agreeable but pessimistic, and parrots me in saying that if she
wants to receive letters and answer them, she'll have to make this
effort.

Elizabeth was once an excellent stenographer. I am showing
her that it is possible to write shorthand with her left hand. We
made up a game today.

I used the letters of the alphabet for both women to work
with. Today we started. Elizabeth wrote four words in shorthand with her *left* hand, words that began with A. She listed
them in a column. In a second column, she drew a picture
of each word. Then, in a third column, Colette was to guess and
print out what each picture represented. Because Colette said
she was not yet prepared to write with her left hand, I
printed in the words as she guessed them. But I deliberately
wrote with my left hand to show Colette and Elizabeth how a
right-handed person can use her other hand.

Saturday, July 31

Today Margaret was out to a ball game with her family and
I used the opportunity to get a discussion going with Mary and
Lillian, Margaret's roommates. We talked about Mary's talents,
and Mary denied having any. I observed that Mary knows everything that is going on in the nursing home, and jokingly suggested
that she ought to be a reporter on the Gazette. I think that
appealed to her.

Later, I spent some five minutes talking to Clara. She seemed
so gracious and grateful for my suggestion that my husband

build a sloping tray for her so she can play bingo lying down.

Thursday, August 5

Worked with Elizabeth and Colette. Colette said she did not want to do anything, but actually she was very cooperative.

We were at the letter B, with Elizabeth writing four words in shorthand beginning with B, and then drawing a picture of each word. As with A of the last time, Colette tried to guess what each picture represented. I started to write down the word that was Colette's guess when Colette herself actually wrote the word alongside mine.

Colette said she found that writing script with her weak and damaged right hand was less effort than printing with her uninjured left hand. I was unbelieving until she told me that she can embroider with her right hand and that her control over her right hand has steadily improved. This is exciting because a few weeks ago when she used her right hand to trace her left, she was very shaky. How much of this is mind over matter I don't know. It certainly is not from physical therapy, which I have not seen any evidence of.

Gertrude, one of Elizabeth's roommates, was in the room with us and, as usual, was attentive but distant. It was she who guessed "Anacin" last week when we were trying to figure out one of Elizabeth's drawings for A. I wonder if Elizabeth chose Anacin because it is part of her medication.

The second part of the hour I devoted to drawing circles on a sheet of paper, each circle representing a member of Elizabeth's family as she recalled them from childhood. I labeled each circle with the family member's name. This will lead to family talk another time.

When I casually asked Gertrude if she had family in this

part of the state, she bristled. "Why are you asking me these
questions? I am not part of your project." I smiled and said
I hoped she would be some day. Later, apropos a remark she
made the other day, I promised Gertrude that I would bring in
some good honey from my neighbor Bill Ilson's hives. No
reaction. (Of course I will have to get the charge nurse's okay
before I bring in the honey. I must remember *not* to turn an
offer into a promise. I cannot make such a promise without
permission.) I suppose the offer was my way of apologizing to
Gertrude for having miffed her.

Saturday, August 7
Lorraine made a medallion in clay.
Margaret made several medallions.
An unexpected session. I had planned on doing pastel work
with Margaret, having a chat with Clara, and doing clay work
with Stanley (a man with no legs who last week asked to
join our group). Clara had company. And Stanley kept
dozing off. Margaret preferred to work with clay. So I worked
with clay with Lorraine and Margaret.

Thursday, August 12
Today I worked with Margaret. I have switched days since
Margaret is not likely to be here this Saturday. She frequently
goes home on weekends. On Saturdays I will work with Colette
and Elizabeth instead.
Margaret made an ashtray, a medallion, and a vase. She
concentrates very well.

Saturday, August 14
Today was good. Colette, objecting all the time, par-

ticipated and carefully watched Elizabeth. We have a nice project going—the entire alphabet. Today we did the letters C, D, E, F, and G. It was Elizabeth's idea that we do more than one letter at a time. We call the project "alphabet sheets."

To remind myself: Get Gregg shorthand textbook from library. Use the basics of the Palmer Penmanship Method to provide exercise for Elizabeth and Colette.

Thursday, August 19

With Margaret. Now that the clay objects have been fired, we picked up where we left off in our ceramic work. Margaret glazed the objects. She was thoroughly occupied and performed excellently.

Until all the pottery is glazed, I expect to work on Thursdays with Margaret and one other person whose work is to be glazed. In the meantime, on Saturdays I will continue to work with Elizabeth in restoring her stenographic and handwriting skills. She is very pleased with herself. No doubt Colette will continue to join us in spite of her feigned objections.

Saturday, August 21

Brought in a shorthand textbook for Elizabeth. She reads shorthand fluently. We are at the letter H. Colette did her part, guessing and writing. She has not said anything yet about writing to her family.

Visited with Mary and showed her the fired pottery.

Mary, Margaret, and Colette will glaze their wares next Thursday. At another time will work with Lorraine, when she glazes her pottery.

Elizabeth and Colette practiced the Palmer method. Big loops and parallel lines. I think it is good exercise. You might call it effortless physical therapy.

Thursday, August 26
[Note from activities director]
Athena, Colette was talking about the glazing she is going to do on Saturday—with relish. I had the impression that having something definite to look forward to was important to her. Elizabeth has been complaining less about things in general.
                                                    —Esther

[Note to activities director]
Oh, Esther, what an encouraging note from you.   *—Athena*

A change of plans for next Saturday: I will not ask Colette to work in Elizabeth's room since it turns out that Ruth (Elizabeth and Gertrude's roommate) finds the presence of Colette in her room disturbing, and since Ruth apparently dislikes Colette and finds her noisy and offensive, I decided to separate my working places and will work with Colette in the sun room for half an hour and then with Elizabeth in Elizabeth's room, thereby including Ruth, even though she has not asked to be included.

I would have liked to have Elizabeth and Colette work together to recapture their writing skills. But no matter. I believe Colette is losing interest. Elizabeth could have come to the sun room but I did not want to give Ruth the power to evict us. However, I also wanted to respect the *dislikes* of a patient. Ruth's was the only negative voice and I suppose I could have overlooked her on the (emotionally) unfair democratic principle of majority rule. But I remember my children being taught by their parents that the "negative vote also counts."

Everything splendid today. Mary glazed her trivet. Margaret

glazed her medallions and her two human figures. Since one of the jars of glaze had its label missing, we are all going to have the surprise of seeing what the color will be after the pieces have been fired.

Saturday, August 28

I worked alone with Colette the first half hour. She glazed her candy dish with no resistance at all, indeed with considerable pleasure. She is no longer interested in the writing and guessing game with Elizabeth.

For the second half hour, Elizabeth and I worked in her room. Amazing how both Ruth and Gertrude, her roommates, participated. Elizabeth continued to work on the alphabet sheets without it being a guessing game. Today we finished the letters I and J, and as usual Elizabeth looked for four words for each letter. Wouldn't you know, Ruth supplied one word, and Gertrude supplied three words, plus explicit directions on how to draw "igloo" and "jelly jar." Gertrude actually drew a jelly jar on her Kleenex. She would not give up the folded tissue but held it in her hand.

It was obviously more than a half hour each that I gave them, but it certainly is worth it. And Ruth was in such a good mood, not having to listen to Colette.

I promised Elizabeth to bring in a strong "something," maybe a stick, instead of the makeshift prop she uses to keep her window open. In that way her long set of tongs can be used for what they were intended—to pick up things that drop on the floor—and not to hold up a window.

Thursday, September 2

Margaret made two dozen clay buttons.

Elizabeth was interested, so I'll combine her two enterprises —making buttons sometimes and continuing with shorthand.

Margaret's very grown son visited and watched us. (I think he's a Selectman). I suggested that he arrange an appointment with me and I can teach him how to use clay so that on weekends at home Margaret might make something. It can be brought back to the nursing home and I'll have it fired. I must look into getting families involved in the creative arts.

Amelia, the woman with one eye and cancer, may yet be one of my people. She was very curious and observed us in a quiet way—not the usual complaining, nervous way that has been characteristic of her.

A very good afternoon it was.

Saturday, September 4
[Note from social worker]
Athena, I thought you would be interested. This afternoon Elizabeth was very engrossed in studying her shorthand textbook.
—Louise
[Note to social worker]
Louise, What an exciting thing to tell me. I'm thrilled.—Athena

Interesting development. Lorraine had made medallions and a candy dish back in June. Today she put the first coat of glaze on them. She held the brush shakily, but actually was able to coordinate her movements, dipping into the jar and dabbing at the pottery. But what do I do about this twist: Lorraine does not remember ever having made those clay objects!

Colette decided to be ornery today and I did not coax her because I wanted to work with Lorraine.

All this was to have taken a half hour but it was closer to an hour. I can't bring myself to count the minutes.

Then I went to Elizabeth for the second half hour. She asked to dictate a letter to me to send to her friend, Miss Kelly in Easthampton. I was very touched. Elizabeth told me she had taken a year to answer this friend's letter and would not be surprised if it took that long for her friend to reply.

We postponed working on the alphabet sheets in order to write the letter to Miss Kelly today. I hate to let a whole week go without Elizabeth and me reestablishing some contact with shorthand. Since the social worker had told me that Elizabeth was reading her shorthand book during the week, I spent an additional twenty minutes today having Elizabeth translate out loud some pages of the library shorthand book that we have borrowed. I will also see Elizabeth this coming Thursday.

Very rewarding afternoon.

I've been here for more than three hours (I was hired to work two hours a week). I will keep track of my overtime, but just for the record.

Thursday, September 9

[Note from social worker]

Athena, Amelia is very occupied with her ailments and I feel that if approached directly to participate in a craft activity she will probably refuse. If, very subtly, you can get her involved, I believe it will be very profitable. She is a very sensitive woman. Good luck. —*Louise*

[Note to social worker]

Louise, I know just what you mean about Amelia. It will take time. —*Athena*

With Elizabeth and Margaret. We spent about fifteen minutes on shorthand and some time on punching two holes in small, round clay circles to make buttons. It was a cooperative effort. Margaret made the flat circles and Elizabeth the holes. It makes me so proud when I see patients cooperating with each other. Lorraine finished two coats of glaze on her objects, two medallions and one candy dish. They are all ready for firing and the finished products should be beautiful.

The buttons are not ready for glazing.

Saturday, September 11
I spent a half hour with Amelia in her room. We talked about her roommate Clara, and her sudden death; and that I had been working on having an angled tray made for Clara so that she could play bingo.

Amelia left her own present miseries for a while and spoke about four deaths within two weeks many years ago, and what a shock they were to her. Two brothers, a sister-in-law, and her husband who hanged himself. Apparently these events led to Amelia having to go to the state hospital, where they gave her shock treatment. I was holding her hand while she described these events to me and she did not pull away.

Amelia is not clear who "Louise" the social worker is. She thought she wore a white uniform and was a nurse. She says she does not know "Esther," and "Athena" is too hard for her to remember, she says. Amelia gave me a brief history of her long connection with the telephone company as a telephone operator.

Colette is waiting for the pottery to come back from the kiln. It has to be fired two times, of course. She does not want to learn to write any better with her right hand anymore. Do I give that project up entirely? I don't know. She says nothing about writing to her family. Nor does she complain about not hearing from them.

With Mary and Lorraine there does not seem any prospect of continuing clay work until the present ceramic pieces return from the kiln. It is a matter of their impatience. It is not the same for Margaret, because she wants to make more ashtrays even while waiting to glaze the buttons.

As for Elizabeth, we have long-range plans. We are up through M in the alphabet, with her writing four words for each letter in shorthand and drawing four corresponding pictures. She is on her own now. But the big thrill today was Gertrude's participation not only in suggesting the drawings for Elizabeth's N words but even in doing a drawing herself. At first Gertrude said, "I said I don't want to be involved," so I quickly removed the paper she was drawing on. But the next minute she was willing to do two more drawings. All of a sudden it feels as though all of us are really working together. It is an exciting feeling for me.

Thursday, September 16
Elizabeth is continuing with her shorthand. Again Gertrude contributed suggestions. A very good hour with them both.

Saturday, September 18
Most of the pottery is finished. I brought them in from the kiln. Elizabeth glazed the dozen buttons in which she had made holes. She held the brush very well. We worked in the sun room and Elizabeth was annoyed at a patient who called out "Hey!" and babbled about preparing dinner. I had never seen Elizabeth cross before. She scolded the patient.

Margaret finished the glaze on her two dozen buttons, an

ashtray which she wants to give to her daughter-in-law, and a medallion. She was pleased with the other work she did that is now finished, including a necklace made out of some of the beads she and Mary had made in June.

Mary was shown her trivet and did not like it or want it. I asked if I could put it on exhibit and she said she didn't care.

I wonder what's going on with Lorraine. She keeps to herself.

Colette is pleased with her candy dish, which she wants to give to her daughter for Christmas.

Amelia watched us. She said she saw no point in making a necklace out of those remaining beads. I will visit with her next Thursday and perhaps get some suggestions from her as to how it could make sense. For one thing, she said the necklace would be too heavy. I pointed out that this is something we all learned, that is, that clay beads have to be small.

[Note to activities director]
Esther, do you know where we can get a nice, old-fashioned china cabinet for articles made by the patients that might be put in the front hall on exhibit? I look forward to showing you and Louise the ceramics when this last batch is finished. —*Athena*

Thursday, September 23

Amelia let me hold her hand while she talked to me for twenty minutes saying she was unhappy. We talked about my possibly reading to her, but that does not interest her. She said her favorite subject in school was spelling, so we are going to put some words together with my Scrabble set.

Elizabeth finished another letter, R, in shorthand and we reviewed her work to date. She was pleased. G and H sheets are missing. I must look for them.

When I met Esther in the hall, she said she would look into getting a china cabinet.

Saturday, September 25

I have been asked if I want to increase my hours from two hours per week to four hours. I agreed, and I made a novel suggestion that was accepted: that my pay be *doubled* for the first two hours, and that the remaining two hours (or more) be gratis. I said that doing it that way would give me the feeling that I was valued. Sometime in the future I may even be glad to come in and work on Sundays gratis because I think it is very important for the morale of those patients who do not have visitors on that day. I can see signs of me as an emerging volunteer rather than as a paid employee.

Although the activities director continues to think of me as an Activities Person, I am not. I have felt right along that if a patient just talked to me, we would be doing something worthwhile. We don't need an "activity."

Margaret must be very fond of her daughter-in-law. She drew pictures today of her family and featured her daughter-in-law first, then her grandchildren, and last, her son.

Thursday, September 30

Elizabeth is finishing the alphabet. She is up to the letter V. Ruth and Gertrude continue to help in making word suggestions.

Saturday, October 2

With Elizabeth. We are now up to W. I feel Gertrude is on the verge of becoming an active participant.

Thursday, October 7

A great deal of participation today.

A lively discussion with Colette and Lorraine about clay work. Colette has her candy dish in her room with candy in it. Lorraine also has her candy dish in her room. I told them that if the clay dishes break, not to throw them out—I will repair them. Lively day. Ruth is an active participant in supplying words for Elizabeth to draw. Today we finished X. It was amusing because we looked words up in the dictionary, and Elizabeth drew Xanthippe, the shrewish wife of Socrates.

We also used the word xylophone, an instrument Elizabeth had never seen. I promised to bring mine in next time. I also promised to bring in an X-ray picture, something else Elizabeth has never seen. As for Xerox, she had heard of it and figured it looked like a box that sat on a table.

On Saturday, Colette, Lorraine, and a new person, Eva (whom Lorraine recognized as a school friend of hers), are all going to work with clay.

Saturday, October 9

Much activity. Brought in my xylophone. Elizabeth played at it. She might get a tune out of it with some practice.

Worked with Eva, who made clay buttons and complained constantly, but I do think she enjoyed the work. She is looking forward to glazing the buttons.

Colette made a medallion and another candy dish, this one for her daughter. She kept referring to the first dish she made, which she was surprised to see turn out so pretty.

Lorraine made buttons.

Eva also made a medallion for one of her granddaughters.

Spent only a few minutes with Elizabeth, but they were pleasant and, as always, she thanked me.

Showed Mary and Margaret what was done today. Margaret commented, "You did a lot today."

Spoke a few minutes to Amelia. I have a bet with her daughter that I will succeed in getting her mother to do something with me. The bet is a cup of coffee. But Amelia turned down the Scrabble spelling connection I had suggested earlier.

Thursday, October 14

With Elizabeth. We finished the alphabet sheets. And we found the lost G and H sheets.

Saturday, October 16

Worked with Colette, Lorraine, and Eva. Colette expressed eagerness to meet with me to make more candy dishes and ashtrays for the rest of her family. She was a lamb today. Made an ashtray for her son and a vase, she's not sure for whom.

Lorraine made imaginative animals, two of them, and a medallion, and a flat something (paperweight, maybe) with her first initial.

Eva made a medallion for another granddaughter, Bamba, with a B on it, and another one for my daughter—H for Hera. That was thoughtful of Eva.

Had a fifteen-minute conversation with Ruth, Gertrude, and Elizabeth. I told them about the dream I had last night of using the nursing-home foyer to display our art work, and Gertrude had a fit. "You watch out—you're like a rambler rose. You're going to take over." But she was good natured about it and I smiled.

I have no idea what Ruth and Elizabeth thought about this.

Eva's two medallions

Thursday, October 21

I showed Margaret her successful ceramic pieces. On Saturday she will glaze them.

Worked with Elizabeth. Now that she has finished the alphabet, she would like to start all over. She wants to write a book. She is going to start an alphabet book with only one illustration for each letter. She wants it to be a book for a child of about four years and will gear her drawings and words to such a child. How ambitious. We did a sample today. The unique aspect of this second project is that since Elizabeth knows shorthand, the shorthand character for a word illustrating a particular letter will be used as a decorative motif around the page as a border design. We examined some of the words that she used in the other completed project. We laughed when we came to X—what will we use? Surely not Xanthippe!

Ruth looked at the sample page we did today, and since she, too, knows shorthand, she thought the border idea was amusing.

Gertrude participated in discussing words which Elizabeth

might use to illustrate the letters, but Elizabeth was not receptive to suggestions.

I find Elizabeth much less diffident than she has been. She exercises some choice in colors now instead of saying, "I don't care." But when Ruth commented, "Too bad the apple was drawn in orange; it would be better in red," Elizabeth agreed with her and said she will consider doing it over again in red.

I did not come to Elizabeth's support, thinking it was more important that she and Ruth were having something to say to each other. I have learned when it is and when it is not important to intervene.

Saturday, October 23

Had a conversation with Sylvia, a nurse, who wanted to know the educational implications of my art instruction. This interaction of staff's curiosity and patients' work is one more positive step towards the diminishing of isolation.

Margaret, Colette, Lorraine, and Eva all put glaze on their clay objects.

Visited briefly with Mary and showed her my mending job on the small oriental rug using the stitch that she taught me. Also visited briefly with Elizabeth and showed her the clay buttons which she had glazed herself. She was pleased.

I explained to Sally, the cook, the progress that Elizabeth is making. Sally too had approached me and wondered if I would please explain the kind of art work the patients are doing. I asked Sally if she remembered how frozen in the wheelchair Elizabeth used to appear to be. Yes, she thought Elizabeth was hunched over her book and maybe even snobbish, unless you'd say she was hard of hearing. I told Sally that I didn't think the *kind* of art work was an explanation for the change she saw in

Elizabeth. Art was only a vehicle. Elizabeth was beginning to develop the self-confidence that had long ago dropped away from her, and little by little her personality was changing.

Thursday, October 28
Starting in November I will work two hours on Thursdays and two hours on Saturdays, from 2:30 to 4:30. Arrangements will be made in January for my working on Sundays also.

The activities director, Esther, arranged a very nice Halloween party with pumpkins used in various ways. There was also a singing program by a group of Girl Scouts.

Because I would not be here this coming Saturday (I had previously arranged to go to an all-day workshop at the Amherst Senior Center on "Arts and the Senior Citizen"), I worked double time today. I did not know that I would be working at cross purposes with the concert program in the sun room already planned by the Girl Scouts. I feel this was nobody's fault but mine (although Esther thinks it was her fault). Since Esther will be leaving pretty soon, I regret that this occasion was spoiled (as I do believe it must have been) by this lack of communication and the crowded situation at the end of the sun room where I was working.

Colette and Eva put glaze on their pottery, and I had a session with Elizabeth about her projected Alphabet Book.

Thursday, November 4
Because of the workshop, I wasn't here Saturday.

Ron, the silent, cigarette-smoking Navy man, apologized as he approached and asked if I could help him with his memory. I was very surprised at his courage and directness. I offered him some clay to start with and said it seemed a good idea if he'd start

working with his hands. We could talk later on. He was willing.
He made an ashtray. Colette made one, too, for her nephew.

Colette's ashtray for her nephew

Saturday, November 6

Ron was reticent and did not want to talk to me today. I
wonder if he scared himself at the prospect of opening up.
He said he did not feel well. Stanley, inspired by Ron's ashtray
the other day, asked to join us. He made a clay ashtray, as did
Margaret and Colette. Eva participated some in cleaning up.

Thursday, November 11

Colette has been anxious about her pottery, afraid it will
explode in the kiln (and of course there is always that possibility). So she was very pleased to see the finished ashtray with
her nephew's name written on it. She showed it off with pride to
people in the sun room. Ron was pleased that his ashtray
survived the kiln. He wants to keep it in his room until

Saturday, when he will glaze it.

Elizabeth worked on the Alphabet Book. She finds she is drawing recognizable objects. The fish for F is very good, she said.

In the earlier project of the alphabet sheets that Elizabeth completed, she used four illustrations for each letter. Some objects were recognizable, some were not. At the time it did not seem to matter. It was an interchange between Elizabeth and Colette: one was drawing, the other was guessing what was drawn.

But in this Alphabet Book, which is specifically intended for a child, Elizabeth is very concerned with the clarity of the drawings.

It may seem strange that a person (forget that her fingers are crippled) who has never drawn in her life could draw such a good FISH. These are the directions I gave her: "Now a fish has a head, almost any shape: curved, pointed, almost square. It has no neck. It has a body that tapers [and my hands make such a gesture], and it might have a fan for a tail. It has scales like a series of the letter U." And this is what she drew:

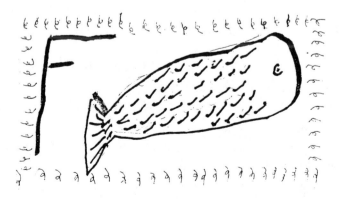

The enthusiasm of Elizabeth was caught by her roommates and manifested itself as good spirits: Gertrude simply borrowed my jacket when I opened the window, instead of complaining about the air as she usually does.

Ruth was almost friendly. Unsolicited, she suggested illustrations to Elizabeth for letters. "Hat" for H. She thought a child would like that. And "Ice" for I.

Saturday, November 13
Hard work today. Stanley was actually the most reluctant. He used the football game on TV as an excuse and begged off at first by saying he was lazy. But when he came around at four o'clock he glazed his ashtray with skill and interest as I held the ashtray for him.

Ron also glazed his ashtray, but he was not able to sit still long enough to finish it at one sitting. He kept getting up from his work to go out for a cigarette. And yet he was very willing and cooperative.

Colette was in a bad mood and needed coaxing to start glazing, but once she started she went on her own momentum.

Eva finished her medallion. Margaret also finished hers.

Ron said he had been a mechanic on industrial machines. We'll see how we can incorporate his knowledge in some clay work.

Too many people today. Very exhausting for me when cajoling and coaxing are necessary.

Ron is willing to do another something next time. "As long as it is nothing practical," he said. We'll see.

I find the nurses showing a continued interest in the work and discussing it with the patients. One nurse had had no idea that there were several steps involved from the clay to the finished object.

Thursday, November 18

This was such a good day. Elizabeth is getting more confidence. She actually chooses a color instead of saying, "It's up to you." She's working on her child's Alphabet Book and has reached the letter J.

I expect to be here Thursday on Thanksgiving and eat with my friends and later continue with our art activities. (My own Thanksgiving is the next day, Friday, when my family will be gathering.) The fact that I might have been overlooking my own family on Thanksgiving Day was of concern to Elizabeth and Gertrude. It was very touching to see the roles reversed: to see a patient's consideration for me.

Saturday, November 20

Margaret has her pottery in her room. So have Colette and Ron and Stanley.

Ruth participated today. She asked to make an ashtray for her husband.

Elizabeth, it seemed to me, felt left out. So I worked on one more letter of the alphabet with her, K.

Ron said he might be willing to do a chart for the kitchen staff, converting measurements into the metric system. He was very pleased with his ashtray and has already used it. He said he would carry it around with him. I did not ask him if he thought the project of converting measurements was "nothing practical," as he expressed it last Saturday.

I had my son take photographs of all the ceramic works and Elizabeth's book, and I would like to exhibit these pictures next year after the holidays are over. Here is one of the pictures:

Photo by Mario Cohn-Haft

Thursday, Thanksgiving

Had noon dinner here, as a guest. Sat with Lorraine, Elizabeth, Stanley, and a man I didn't know. Delicious meal. Lovely cooperative attitude on everybody's part.

The administrator took a picture of Elizabeth for me.

Worked entirely with Elizabeth from one to three p.m. Guests came to visit Gertrude. It turns out that I've known her son for ten years now as an excellent butcher in our town. Her nephew is a psychologist. I showed him Elizabeth's work. He teased his aunt by saying she ought to work with me.

Saturday, November 27

Lorraine met me in the hall and said, "Hi, lady." She says she recognizes me but does not remember my name. I gave her my arm and we went for a walk outdoors around the building. She said she wished she was dead, but did not enlarge on it. When we came in, I invited her to do some clay work. She made a candlestick by herself, and a pinch bowl with a great deal of help from me. She also sat and read several pages of a ceramic textbook.

I believe she was pleased with her work. We showed it off to Stanley and Ron, who were polite.

Ruth liked Lorraine's work and expressed a desire to make a candlestick, which we did today. She had come up to me earlier to ask if her ashtray survived its firing. I told her that I didn't know yet and promised to phone her when I found out.

Gertrude talked to me about playing jacks when she was a girl, and we compared notes about that.

I remember now that Lorraine said she had worked in the dry goods section of a department store years ago in Northampton.

I asked Elizabeth if she wanted to work with clay, but she said she would prefer to get on with the Alphabet Book. I stayed late just for her to finish the letter O. I was very pleased that Elizabeth stated clearly what she wanted to do.

Sylvia, the nurse, has been promised some buttons by Elizabeth and me. She loves the idea.

Thursday, December 2

Extraordinary sense of rapport in Elizabeth's room with Ruth and Gertrude and me. Margaret came in, too, and watched Elizabeth work on her Alphabet Book. Letters P, Q, R, S, and T today.

I showed them my son's photographs of their ceramic work.

Everybody was enthusiastic.

Saturday, December 4

Worked with Elizabeth instead of Ruth because the kiln lady was not home and I couldn't pick up Ruth's ashtray. Ruth will glaze it next Thursday. I was glad to see how concerned she was to have the ashtray finished in time for Christmas. That she still cares is gratifying.

Excellent day. Elizabeth went as far as W in the alphabet. This time she was showing signs of considerable independence. She accepted Gertrude's suggestion of "umbrella" for U, but rejected her suggestions for V, and drew a vase.

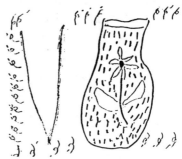

The V page is the first work done *entirely* by Elizabeth. I have been drawing the guidelines—at first all four borders, then recently just the top and bottom borders and Elizabeth would connect my lines. This time, for V, she drew all the guidelines by herself and decorated her vase drawing without any suggestions from me.

Whenever Elizabeth has to draw an object and she says she cannot, which is always, I describe it to her. For instance, for "vase" I raise my two hands and say, as I draw shapes in the air, that starting from the top there is the top of the vase; it probably has a neck that is narrower than the top; and then it can bulge for the body until it reaches its base, which would probably be resting on a surface. And that is how she regularly proceeds.

Only in one instance do I recall my actually drawing and her

copying what she asked me to draw. That was "dog" for D.
I drew a head upside down on a piece of scrap paper facing Elizabeth and pointed out that the head merges with the body
and from the body four legs descend and a tail is attached. Then
back to the head, where you can see one eye in profile and
the ear, which can go up or down. She chose down.
Then she copied that picture and it is the least interesting
of all her drawings. All others have been from verbal
descriptions and my hands shaping the object in the air in
front of us both. The interesting thing is that drawing from what
one sees in one's mind's eye is often easier than copying an object
in front of one.

Thursday, December 9
When I arrived in Ruth's room, she had dozed off. I
hesitated to awaken her, although Gertrude encouraged me to.
Instead, I worked with Elizabeth, and she illustrated one
letter, X. She seemed tired and tense. When it came to doing the shorthand as a border design, she said softly, "Oh, dear."
Don't know if she felt pressed or what. She didn't like her
shorthand representation of the word "Xerox." She wasn't
sure a four-year-old would understand "Xerox" anyway, but she
found it pretty sophisticated to be drawing something so
modern as a machine she had never seen, something she had
only heard of.
When Ruth woke up, she glazed her ashtray. I asked her to
also glaze a little ceramic squirrel as an experiment, using
thawed-out glaze that had frozen in my car. I deliberately
asked her to do this so (1) we could learn what effect one
gets from using frozen and thawed-out glaze, and (2) she could
participate in the experiment to determine this information.

Ruth said she was "bored" as she was glazing. But she did stir the jar, and she followed directions to extract tiny crystal lumps from the jar and place them on her piece. The more lumps of crystal, the prettier her ceramic piece would be, we thought.

I went back and forth between Ruth and Elizabeth. I had the feeling that they were both miffed at me for dividing myself up.

It was so hot in Ruth and Elizabeth's room that I apologized for taking off my heavy lined boots and working in woolen socks. I felt a certain discomfort, as though I, by being eccentric, was taking some attention away from both women.

At 4:30 I was bushed.

Saturday, December 11

Eva wanted to make an ashtray for her son-in-law. Which she did.

Elizabeth worked on her book and said she would be relieved when it was finished. I don't understand what that indicates. She criticizes her lack of control of her shorthand writing. She seems to be a perfectionist.

So far, drawing is a good medium for Elizabeth. She can both express and camouflage her feelings. This was the case when she drew a rather crotchety type like Gertrude M. to illustrate the letter M and called it "Mrs. M." Gertrude protested the resemblance to herself and the use of her last initial.

Elizabeth then changed the drawing's expression by adding a smile to become a drawing of Margaret instead. She called it "Margaret L." Margaret was pleased. The turned-up smile did the trick. In the drawing, Elizabeth withdrew her feelings of irritation toward Gertrude; instead, she expressed her feelings of respect for Margaret.

Elizabeth's drawing of Margaret instead of Gertrude—everybody pleased.

Colette was quiet. She watched Eva work and admired her ashtray. Colette complained that the green color of the dish she made for her daughter was the only pretty color, and she wished she had not made the others so plain.

Margaret decided how she would distribute the things she had made. She gave me two figurines as a present. When I reminded her that Sylvia, the nurse, had admired the ceramic buttons, she asked that Sylvia be called. Sylvia accepted three buttons and said she would sew them on her sweater. Margaret was pleased.

Thursday, December 16
Elizabeth finished up with Z. She applied herself very intensely and there seems to be greater freedom of movement in her drawing. I don't think this represents an improvement in her physical condition, but it does indicate less awkwardness and timidity in undertaking something for which she clearly thinks she has no ability. For instance, she still feels she cannot draw; and yet, without hesitation, she drew a zinnia with

concentric petals as described to her.

Margaret gave three of her buttons to Sylvia.

Saturday, December 18

I invited Elizabeth to spend Christmas at my house. She accepted. The Medi-Van will pick her up for nothing. We discussed her various nursing-home experiences today. Also her view of what this institution is like.

The day went well. Elizabeth worked very hard making a list of books that she wants the librarian at the Northampton library to send her.

She also worked on the title page of her book, which was tentatively called *ABC.*

I spent some time with Amelia, who from her experience as a telephone operator discussed the reasons why a telephone call might be intercepted. I'm sorry we've not been able to do anything with her love of spelling. She put me off with not "being in the mood." I guess I've lost my coffee bet with her daughter.

Colette introduced me to her daughter and we three talked about Christmas presents and how the daughter is looking forward to seeing the present Colette made for her.

Gertrude participates on a regular basis now. Her parting words to me today were, "And do you remember now where you are to meet your son?" (Previously, a nurse had come in with a telephone message telling me where to meet him.) At first I said automatically, "At Forbes Library," and she corrected me: "No, at Tom's house." I find her concern with what goes on around her very pleasant. She defended herself when I mentioned this to her and said, "Some people call me nosey." I dismissed that comment. We shook hands as usual when I left. I love being "mothered" by a patient.

Thursday, December 23

Elizabeth finished up her book project. In shorthand she drew lovely "designs" on the cover of her Alphabet Book. What she actually wrote in shorthand that looked like a design was:

Now is the time for all good men to come to the aid of the party. This is a different kind of party. This is a book to amuse a child.

We made tentative plans for future work. Possibly she will write another book.

Gertrude was very talkative. All about her daughter who is divorced, remarried, and very happy.

Saturday, Christmas Day
[Note to social worker]
Louise, I was here for Christmas lunch. Elizabeth asked for a rain check for my Christmas invitation to my house. Worked in the morning. If you look in Elizabeth's folder, you'll see a Christmas tree that she drew and decorated. At first we both agreed that decorations were monotonous until I asked her to draw words in shorthand on the drawing of the tree and I circled each word, making it a bulb hanging from a branch. The result is very decorative.

I am trying to stimulate her powers of observation. When she said she did not know what words to write, I asked her to look at whatever was within sight—my hand, a watch, freckles, a scratch, a color, and so on.

Since I don't know Gregg shorthand, she may have written some personal words. I did not ask her.   *—Athena*

Thursday, December 30
What a successful day! I worked with Lorraine and Eva. Got them each to use colored pens for drawing and coloring.

I gave Lorraine her medallion, which she does not remember making. She is wearing it. Also lent a patient (Megan) another medallion that Lorraine made.

Eva did some drawing, tracing her medallions and then copying the design. It was very difficult for her. She made a tiny "B" instead of the large one that was the actual design. When we measured it, she was able to see the difficulty and felt satisfaction only when she finished tracing all her three medallions. Tracing is like the first step for her. More imaginative work later on.

I spoke to Lillian, who rarely greets me. Her nose was operated on last Monday, as was mine for a possible skin cancer, and our stitches have just been removed. We compared notes and the coincidence of our operations. I guess I use *any* subject just to establish contact.

Did a lot of talking to individuals.

Elizabeth decided not to design any more tree decorations. In her practical way, she was satisfied to have made it through Z in her alphabet book.

Once the ice of withdrawal is broken,
the visual arts often blend with or yield
to other modes of communication,
of which speech is one.

SECOND YEAR

Saturday, January 1

Talked with Elizabeth and Gertrude.

Got signatures on a card to go with the goodbye present we are making for Esther. Lorraine worked hard at trying to make a decorative outline around her name, for whatever reason. Maybe just for the fun of it. Seemed out of breath when she finished.

Colette is ill and does not want to use her bum hand.

Amelia refused to sign, saying she can't see and can't do anything.

Sunday, January 2

Came in for an hour. Quite a bit of talking. Elizabeth and Gertrude seemed very glad to see me. Elizabeth said she had been wondering if I would come in. I find that kind of pessimistic whining very sweet. It just reestablishes contact.

More signatures. Today Amelia actually signed her name, using my finger as a guide.

Started reading *Houses for the Dead* by Ann Turner to Elizabeth, who thinks she will be interested. Explained to Elizabeth my own interest in making peace with myself and my mortality. It interested her. She was also interested that Ann Turner is my stepdaughter.

Thursday, January 6

Louise, the social worker, dropped in on me and I was very pleased. I showed her Elizabeth's ABC book. I told her

I'd like to have a show in February of photographs of the clay work the patients have done and photocopies of some pages of Elizabeth's alphabet book.

Saturday, January 8
Spoke to Megan. She told me about having once been a bookkeeper, and said she would like to work with numbers. Eva has bronchitis. I did not work with her as I had hoped.

Thursday, January 13
Megan obliged me by writing words that someone might use to illustrate a future alphabet book. She acted as though she was willing to do it for me but not for herself. Firm handwriting. Interesting selection of words: *And, Beautiful, Cave, David, Eat, Four, Garb, Heroes, Isaac, Just, Kangaroo, Little, Mother, Not, Otter, Pop*, and that's where she stopped.

She said she was hungry and I got two saltines for her. She went back and worked with confidence and speed. *Qua* (Latin), *Rise, Santa Claus, Table, United, Vogue, William, Xyz, You, Zoo.*

One of the nurses (Doris, a very sweet girl) had an unfortunate conversation, I thought, with Annie, one of the very old patients. The nurse scolded Annie for having torn pages out of a book. I offered to bring in a book that could be torn, like an old telephone book, but Annie turned on me saying, "I'm not that kind of lady." I don't know what she meant by that. Then Doris, just to make conversation perhaps, after admiring the work of Megan, turned to Annie and said, "Annie, can you write?" Annie turned on her and said,

"What an awful thing to ask. A woman who has raised three children." It was almost too much. First a reproach for tearing a book and then that mindless question.

When Doris walked off, I went over to Annie, took her hands and agreed with her: "What an awful thing to say." I told her I had three children, too. I was pleased that I was able to help Annie express her distress.

When I first came in at 2:30, I spent ten minutes or so with Gertrude and Elizabeth. We talked about the ways religion and death are discussed in the book, *Houses for the Dead*. Gertrude was particularly interested in talking about "souls" and how her Irish mother would open the window in the room where a dead person·was, to allow the soul to escape.

One of the patients was wheeled up to the table where Margaret and I were working and she was told, "Don't touch anything," by a young, otherwise sensitive nurse. The poor thing mumbled and, like a child, repeated "Don't touch nothing." So I gave her something "to touch," a felt-tipped pen and paper, and asked her to draw a picture. She said she couldn't. But she said she would write her name, and she did some interesting scribbles. She also scribbled her husband's name, but it was illegible. I feel, however, that I salvaged a little dignity for her.

Saturday, January 15

Brought in a book for Elizabeth, *The Arthritic's Cookbook*. I feel the Introduction is very encouraging and, although I don't want to get Elizabeth's hopes up, I think it will give her pleasure to know there is help for some people, at least. I, too, am supposed to have arthritis, but when the doctor told me I should take twelve aspirins a day, I said nothing doing. So

I am going to try the diet for myself. I discussed this with Elizabeth and I think this is another bond between us.

While Elizabeth was reading the book (I told her I was lending it to her, so there was no need to hurry), I spent an hour with Colette.

Colette told me some very impressive stories about herself. How when she was in her early thirties with five children at home (the oldest ten years of age), she, her husband, and their in-laws went for a drive. Her husband fell out of the moving car and when they drove back to where he was lying, he was dead. She has a lot of grit, Colette has. Not even a tear as she was telling me the story.

So she learned how to earn a living for herself and her children. She went to a beauty school at night for eight months and then opened a beauty shop in her apartment, and that was that.

Very impressive to me. I like her. And I think she knows this. I am becoming what is called an "active listener," and I feel privileged. I want to work out a program for her.

Thursday, January 20

It was Inauguration Day and Elizabeth preferred to watch the inauguration on TV rather than work with me.

Lorraine was wandering around and I invited her to sit and talk with me. Just to loosen her up, I asked her to draw circles traveling across the page. The concept was too difficult since a traveling circle is the same as a spiral. So she drew concentric circles and thought the very center of the circle looked like a baby. Later when she looked at the drawing she thought it resembled a clam shell.

We went from drawing the concentric circles to talking about

Lorraine's childhood and family. She drew a circle for each family member, leaving her father out until I asked her to draw a circle for him, too. She said he was a very kind and quiet man. He moved things around at the Clarke School for for the Deaf, and he loved the deaf children.

Lorraine made a list of all the children in the family, putting an X alongside those who had died, and she came up with eight. She said she was child No. 7; there were eight children and two were born after her. That presented a problem of addition. The ninth child was discussed although I was not interested in whether or not there was a ninth child. There is a time and place for inaccuracy.

I feel it is important that she remember her early family as a starting point for remembering anything, and it is these recollections that I hope to be working on with her. That Lorraine might be remembering inaccurately does not matter to the process of her re-establishing a connection with the world.

Thursday, January 27

Today Ron went through the alphabet with me, giving me a naval or sea word for each letter. We might do an alphabet book. He says he does not know how to draw, but he has done mechanical drawing.

Amelia did not want to talk to me.

Lorraine drew an apple in sections.

Elizabeth has a cold and feared she might give it to me if I worked with her, so we postponed our work to Saturday.

Saturday, January 29

With Mary. She would not draw. But she told me the names of the members of her family, and I drew a circle for each of them.

Gave Elizabeth instructions in copying—not tracing. We used a flower design of my scarf, and it was a lesson in observation—noticing the direction of the petals, the number of petals, their color, background, the border, and so on.

I can trace Elizabeth's drawing and put it on a backing so that some other patient can do the needlework using Elizabeth's original drawing. Eventually others may work up courage to do their own drawing as a needlework pattern.

Elizabeth is willing to work with Mary, so for Mary this would be very different from her usual loner activities.

Thursday, February 3

I photocopied two copies of Elizabeth's ABC book. I am asking Elizabeth to color in the illustrations on the photocopied copies, and I'll use one of them for demonstration. If Elizabeth wants, she can give away the other copy to whomever she chooses.

If I were to simply ask her to color a coloring book, she would be insulted, considering it childish; but coloring her own book is a source of pride, though the distinction is subtle.

Saturday, February 5

Elizabeth is coloring all the photocopied pages of her book. It is strenuous work, but I find she is exerting herself with pleasure.

She has the strain and exercise of opening each pen. I said I would help if she needed help. I don't believe she thought she could pull off the cover of a pen. Applied "physical therapy," you might say.

Thursday, February 10

I colored photocopied pages of Elizabeth's ABC alphabet book together with her. Colette extremely friendly. Clay work promised for Stanley. A great deal of warm response from a dozen or so residents. This is probably due to the fact that they know that Louise, the social worker, is leaving at the end of the month; several have expressed fear that I might leave, too.

Saturday, February 12

Spread myself out.

Colette asked to examine Elizabeth's book. She liked it. Elizabeth, of course, is pleased to see it viewed.

Lillian said she might as well do a book with me, and we started one.

Mary asked to see Elizabeth's book. She liked it.

Elizabeth finished coloring another one of the photocopies.

Don't know why, but it felt unsettled today. Perhaps I worked with too many people. There is a point of diminishing returns even in human service.

Thursday, February 17

Stanley made a clay horse. He has inoperable cataracts. Eighty-eight years old. Wasn't feeling well, reluctant to work.

Ron unwilling to work in clay or continue his own alphabet book.

Only Elizabeth cooperated today. She finished coloring another of the photocopies of her book.

Saturday, February 19

Margaret lived in Flushing, New York, as a girl. So did I,

as a little girl. Another point of contact for us. We write notes to each other. I write to her because, of course, she is pretty deaf, but I ask her to write to me just for the practice of hanging on to her writing skills.

Elizabeth is bedridden. Visited with her. She asked me questions about myself. Sad atmosphere here today.

Thursday, February 24

An exhibit of the work of patients has been postponed indefinitely.

New social worker—Osa.

Gertrude cut paper into small sheets to be used for Elizabeth's next book. Engrossed for over an hour. A nurse came in and said, "You even have Gertrude working!"

That was gauche. I ignored it.

Elizabeth used a form—a stencil that I made for her to draw rectangles on the pages of her blank sheets. The rectangles will serve as frames for her drawings.

Hard work for all. But what was rewarding to me was the successful cooperative effort.

Saturday, February 26

Gertrude cut out more blank paper for Elizabeth's future book.

I mended a prayer book for Elizabeth with Scotch Tape.

Colette spoke about the stifling feeling of listening to two patients (Lorraine is one of them) talking to each other. Makes her feel that she is going crazy. But at least she does not share a room with them, she said.

Thursday, March 3

Elizabeth asleep. Also Gertrude. Visited briefly with Stanley.

Colette colored a heavy legal-size envelope with advertising on it, crossing the words out with different Magic Markers. It ended up making a beautiful envelope with rainbow colors. Will continue on this tack. Don't know where I got this camouflage idea from.

Saturday, March 5
It's exciting. Elizabeth did some camouflage work on a heavy legal-size envelope, blotting out, decoratively, the advertisements. Very fluid results. Spoke to Dr. Olds and showed him Elizabeth's work. Will meet with him later to discuss patients and their limitations based on their drug intake.

Thursday, March 10
Am beginning to understand my own style. I walked straight into Elizabeth's room and saw her sitting in her wheelchair with her right foot in a basin of water. I greeted Gertrude and Ruth, her roommates, and then squatted down and said to Elizabeth, "Oh, my goodness. You're in trouble." I never say, "Hello, Elizabeth, how are you?" I dive right into the situation. Nor do I ask for a health explanation. We talked about Dr. Olds, who had visited Elizabeth, and about her foot that had split open. I gathered it was a kind of bed sore.

I conduct my conversations in Elizabeth's room almost always sitting on her bed. But I first ask her if I may sit on her bed. I never take it for granted.

I said to Elizabeth that I had just made a lot of promises and that I'd better go into the office and quickly write them down. I recited them: 1) to bring clay for Margaret, 2) to say hello to Ron, 3) to work again with Colette on coloring our own pop art by obliterating the advertisements on a heavy legal-size envelope.

After I listed them, Elizabeth said, "Why don't you stay here and write your notes?" That pleased me, and I accepted. Then I went to Colette's room where she was lying down, saying she was dizzy. The nursing home was hot. I asked Colette, who is always cold, if she minded if I opened the window. Then I asked the same of her roommate, who reluctantly gave me permission. I visited with them for a while when Colette suddenly agreed to go into the sun room so that she and I might work together.

As we left the room, I offered to close the window, but Colette's roommate said she would close it herself if necessary. This is exactly what I aim for all the time: to see a dependent person take the initiative. The roommate would close the window when she was ready.

[Am making this report particularly detailed because it came to me suddenly that I have a special technique with patients and I am trying to analyze it. I act as though I am merely visiting people. And then some work does emerge. But I think it is more important that I be a friend than that I be a teacher. This has developed by itself and I like it this way.]

It is interesting about Colette. She says she wants to "work." She does not like wasting her time. For the most part her right hand is shot—it trembles and is flattened out and flabby. Still, she can hold a pen and she does some needlework when her hand is not hurting. She has not tried to write a letter. She must have her reasons.

Colette colored (or colored-out, if you can call it that) all the ads on a legal-size envelope, supplementing some of the work that Elizabeth had done on that same envelope. (I ask them to put their initials under the work they do.)

Working on the legal-size envelope, Colette chose her colors. But she used little imagination at first in blocking out the printed words. After doing four lines on the envelope, including the spaces between the words, in a single color, I suggested that she choose another color. She was, in effect, doing bands of colors. After a bit she confined herself to the words alone and the spaces between bands of color, and in between the bands of color she filled in with circles. I suggested vertical shapes but she was satisfied with circles.

There was one advertisement left when I started to pick up and leave. Colette said she would like to do that one, too. Altogether, she worked for an hour.

Now, is this "work" a legitimate form of occupation? Is the person being treated as a child?

Was Elizabeth's coloring the photocopies of her ABC books also a childish way of spending time? Absolutely not.

What is accomplished by these repeated strokes? Exercise, relaxation, concentration, activity for its own sake, control, exercising the right to reject, and, finally, making something pretty. Ads are often ugly. We blot them out and in the process we might even succeed in making a design that could be very attractive if it were looked at as merely design. It has no objective meaning. The most it has is in the choice of colors and shapes, a subjective meaning, which we do not get to discuss.

I do creative-arts work using whatever I have available as an educational tool. How can we make do with something that apparently does not lend itself to any change, like a printed advertisement?

And in this way I feel that I help an imprisoned person modify his immediate environment.

I went to see Margaret, just to say hello. I had with me an article on poetry writing and I had the feeling that Margaret would be able to write poetry. I showed her the article and asked her to read it. Margaret will do anything she is asked. I picked up the article later when I walked past her room and saw it folded on her end table. I imagine she had read only the first page, simply because I had not made a point of saying there was more beyond that page. Anyhow, she bobbed her head as I reached for the article and she indicated that she was pleased. Perhaps at another time I can sit next to her and we can read it together. Since she is deaf, there is no point in my reading it to her out loud.

When I'm in Margaret's room, I always stop to touch Mary's hand or shoulder or squat down and chat with her with our eyes on the same level. I also chat a bit with Lillian, who ordinarily indicates she wants a conversation by commenting on how busy I am.

Saturday, March 12

Brought clay for Elizabeth. She can actually roll a small ball if she places it on top of her right hand. She made ten balls, probably to be a string of Greek worry-beads.

I opened windows in the sun room, to the pleasure of Colette and Ron. A nurse ran in and closed them, according to the charge nurse's wishes, she said. People will get sick and nurses will have to take care of them, is literally what was said. But I had also opened the sun room door to the outside, and it remained open. Gertrude was very nervous about the possibility of people walking out. I asked Ron and Colette to keep an eye on the door, which they were willing to do. And nobody even tried to walk out. I enjoyed turning over some responsibility to the patients.

Thursday, March 17
Megan and I talked about her days as a bookkeeper. At the same time I was helping Margaret make a clay vase. The two activities did not interfere with each other because Margaret is deaf and so was not disturbed by my conversation with Megan. It was Margaret's idea to make a vase. I will send it to the kiln soon. Her comment was, "It's ugly now but it will be pretty when it's finished."

Sunday, March 20
I was snowed in at home after Friday's storm and could not get out yesterday.

Today: TV carried St. Patrick's Day parade, and in spite of that I was able to get the attention of Ron for about an hour. He did not want to illustrate his nautical alphabet. He did dictate some of his own poetry to me, which I wrote down. He said he would like me to show it to him next week to see if he remembers any of it. He says he has no memory and would like to be able to remember.

Writing poetry may well be a technique for recapturing in metaphors some fleeting thoughts in preparation for less fleeting but more concealed thoughts, perhaps. It's entirely up to him. At one point I asked him if he felt trapped. And when he said yes, I dropped the poetry writing and we talked about dancing. That was a shot in the dark, a way of getting off an unpleasant subject. He said he was once a very good dancer. Somehow I was not surprised.

He would like to know how long he has been here in the nursing home. It seems like months, he said, not years. I will find out for him.

Thursday, March 24

Colette disgruntled—I don't know why. She did a decorative page using her own name. Elizabeth transcribed some poems into shorthand.

Thursday, April 14

Two weeks not here. Back today.

Working with Elizabeth. She will transcribe (into shorthand) for herself excerpts of Dr. Alex Comfort's book on old age, *A Good Age.*

Saturday, April 16

Worked with various people.

With Elizabeth. We just talked. Told her that I have a new schedule—Saturdays and Sundays from 2:30-4:30. I'll not be working on Thursdays any more because I have a second job (part-time) with the Council on Aging in Williamsburg. What happens to my offer to work on Sundays gratis? Well, it will keep, I'm sure.

Visited Colette. She likes to read love stories, she told me. I asked her if she would like to read a book in her native French. Yes, she would. So I will borrow such a book for her. At the moment all I have at home is a French Baedeker.

Stopped for a few minutes with Amelia. She says she is sicker than ever. Can't eat because her gums hurt her.

Stopped to visit everybody in Mary's room. Johanna has

been very ill for three weeks and wants to die, Mary said. Johanna greeted me lucidly and asked about my mother. Then she said she had to go to the bathroom. But since she was restrained in her chair, I called the nurse. Unfortunately, Johanna was not able to wait. I helped the nurse clean up. Johanna does not like to be restrained in her chair. Why is she? I suppose they are afraid she will fall out. But there are chairs like the one Mary has that act as restraints because of the attached table. These are scarce. They have *no business* being scarce. Something to be looked into.

I left a ball of clay with Margaret to experiment with during the week.

Sunday, April 17
Johanna is so ill. Talked with her and her roommates, Mary, Margaret, and Lillian. Mary is particularly upset by her roommate's distress.

Saturday, April 23
Elizabeth remarked that it seemed a long time from one Saturday to the next, now that I don't come in on Thursdays any more.

We read together from the introduction to Comfort's book, *A Good Age.* I read aloud and she listened intently. No comments. Megan walked in and out of the room.

Elizabeth continues to be interested in transcribing Comfort's book. For her, it is practice in a skill that is part of her past.

I am beginning to see that expression for its own sake is not what I can expect from my patients. Instead, I want to help them recapture a lost or forgotten skill and continue to use it.

That may be a dead end. I don't know. Elizabeth's shorthand is being used creatively, as in the alphabet book. What satisfaction is there for her in just transcribing the excerpts of this book on old age? Perhaps an acceptable way of reading on an almost taboo subject.

I asked Elizabeth if she understood her rights with respect to her Social Security checks—that she can dispose of the leftover money herself. She did not know this. She does not have a will and is interested in having one. This means getting in touch with Western Massachusetts Legal Services.

Sunday, April 24
Colette read to me from my French-language Baedeker's *Paris*. She was pleased.

Saturday, April 30
Clay work with Margaret.
Spoke to Colette.

Sunday, May 1
Continued reading aloud the introduction of Dr. Comfort's book to Elizabeth. She will continue to transcribe it in bits and snatches, starting next Saturday.

Showed Mary how to hook a rug with a "plunging" tool. She agreed to try to do it herself next Saturday.

Saturday, May 7
Talking session. Mary very upset about three nursing-home deaths within two weeks. Johanna, one of them. Spoke to Colette, Elizabeth, and Gertrude. Perhaps a memorial service would help soften the shock everyone feels about these deaths.

Sunday, May 8
Clay work with Margaret. No work with Elizabeth. No work with Mary. Depressing day.

Saturday, May 14
Excellent rapport with Elizabeth. She transcribed into shorthand some more of Comfort's *A Good Age*. Read random chapters at Elizabeth's request.
Gertrude expressed disapproving views. She thought Comfort had it all wrong.

Sunday, May 15
Read to Elizabeth. She transcribed some more.

Saturday, May 21
Elizabeth very interested in Comfort's book, particularly the chapters on quacks and medication.
Gertrude borrowed my deck of cards and played solitaire.

Sunday, May 22
Read to Elizabeth. She is such a pleasant and appreciative woman. She transcribed another paragraph of *A Good Age* into shorthand. Then she asked me to read to her from a novel she is reading. Any connection I make with a patient, I appreciate.

Saturday, May 28
Have a plan for Elizabeth, another way to use her shorthand. I am looking for a pen pal for her in another nursing home with whom she can correspond. Will work on this.
In the meanwhile, I am providing Elizabeth with an educat-

ed attitude toward herself and toward old people. Now we are reading *You and Your Aging Parent* by Silverstone and Hyman.

Sitting alongside her, I have been reading aloud and she follows it with her eyes. She stopped me once when there was a reference to medication that she used to take and no longer does. She questioned the advisability of asking Dr. Olds if she should resume it. I asked her for permission to talk to Dr. Olds on her behalf. She gave it to me.

I laughed because Gertrude thinks I am a meddler. When I told her my intentions were good, she was quick to reply, "You know, the way to hell is paved with good intentions." I do like Gertrude.

Sunday, May 29

Elizabeth wrote a letter in shorthand to a woman I know who will read her letter and answer her in shorthand. This is Betty Waller, a retired businesswoman living in Northampton who is very happy to have a correspondence with Elizabeth.

Saturday, June 4

Margaret and Elizabeth glazed their own ceramic work: Elizabeth's ten buttons and Margaret's candy dish and candle holder.

Sunday, June 5

Elizabeth once asked me to bring mending tape for her religious tract, which is falling apart. I brought that packing-wrapping Scotch Tape and mended the book.

I left her with something to read while I went off to see

Eva. The book I left is the one she and I are reading, *You and Your Aging Parent.*

I tried to distract Eva, who calls "Nurrrsse" all day. I asked her to dictate a letter to a friend. She thought it was an insane request, but she complied and we wrote a letter to her sister-in-law, which I will mail. Perhaps Eva will receive an answer. Letter writing is such easy therapy. It's a wonder it's not on top of the list.

Saturday, June 11
With Lillian. We discussed Margaret, her roommate. It appears that Margaret is always restless, going back and forth from the bed to the chair. Lillian felt free to talk in front of Margaret, she being so very deaf.

I believe I shall start reducing the amount of time I spend with Elizabeth and will regularly spend more time with Margaret, working in clay, which she enjoys. Her face lights up when she is so occupied. However, today she only wanted to watch me. I sculpted a man's head, the size of my fist; put a smile on his face; then pushed in his nose and changed his expression. Nice to hear Margaret laugh.

I feel that I have made and am sustaining many inroads with the following people: Gertrude, Margaret, Elizabeth, Colette, Lorraine, Mary, and Lillian.

Mary accepted a book on nursing homes and thumbed through it for a few minutes. She usually refuses any "propaganda" such as Comfort's *A Good Age* or Kübler-Ross's *Death and Dying.*

Stanley goes out of his way to greet me. And Ron is less shy these days.

Eva was so nervous. Kept asking me about her doctor

appointments. Poor thing.

Sunday, June 12
Well, a good day. I have a book, *Nursing Homes*, by Horn and Griesel. Elizabeth chose chapters she wanted me to read to her.

Time flew.

I took Eva out for an ice-cream cone. I also bought a container of ice cream for Lorraine, and when I returned I saw Ron outside. I produced two spoons and he and Lorraine ate from the same container. That was cozy.

Saturday, June 18
Elizabeth still asks to be read to. We are reading about depression in women. She finds it interesting and asks me many questions. I wonder if she opens up with others.

Sunday, June 19
Spent an hour with Eva teaching her some elementary needlework, something she had never done before.

Read to Elizabeth for an hour. She is very interested in the psychological types of women that we have been reading about in a book on depression in women, by De Rosis. Elizabeth has very sophisticated taste it seems to me. I enjoy her responses to the books that I bring in.

Saturday, June 25
Elizabeth received an answer in shorthand from Betty Waller in Northampton. Today Elizabeth is answering her letter.

Sunday, June 26
Dismal day, partly the weather. Felt I wasn't reaching anybody—not even Elizabeth.

Saturday, July 2
Elizabeth helped me put her pennies in bank rolls.
I read to her from the first chapter of *Knowing Women*.

Sunday, July 3
Not feeling well. Turned around and went back home.

Saturday, July 9
I was glad to speak to Osa, the new social worker, during the week.
Will be doing bean prints (a novel artistic use of shelled dried beans) with Elizabeth next time.
Brought ice cream again (with nurse's permission) for Colette, Mary, Gertrude, Elizabeth, and me.

Wednesday, July 20
Another shorthand letter from Elizabeth to Mrs. Waller.
Last day here until August 15. I'll accompany my mother to New York City on a plane and meet my sister at the airport, and my sister and she will fly out to Los Angeles together.

[Note from social worker]
Athena, Your work with Elizabeth has had just fine results. She is much more interested in what is going on here and is a willing participant. —Osa

Wednesday, August 17
Returned to work. Glad to be back.

Rushing out in a hurry to return my rented car before they charge me for another day, and so I'll not write in this notebook today.

Saturday, August 27
I'll be working only one day a week for a while because my other job (as senior aide in the Williamsburg Council on Aging) is pretty demanding. Four hours on Saturdays.

Saturday, September 3
Today was great. I must try to get an Elvis Presley record for Elizabeth and borrow a player. I gave her a picture of Elvis. He is one of her heroes.

Elizabeth asked me to help her write a letter to her lawyer pertaining to a funeral plot for herself. Isn't it interesting that she is so calm about this?

She has been writing and receiving letters from Mrs. Waller.

I can't begin to say how pleased I am with Elizabeth (to say nothing of Mrs. Waller).

[Note to social worker]
Osa, Elizabeth said it's OK for you to see the letters to and from Mrs. Waller, so I am leaving her file on the desk. Will pick it up next week.   *—Athena*

Saturday, September 10
I'll have to switch next week to Sunday.

Margaret made a collage of a flower, with wool and beans. It's on her dresser and she is going to give it to her daughter-in-law.

Elizabeth made a collage of a butterfly out of beans. Elizabeth and Margaret both seemed pleased with their work. Elizabeth pushed the beans with a pencil. She asked me to spread the glue. She made some conversation as she worked, asking me about the vegetables I freeze. (This bean business is not exactly my speed, but clearly it is fun.) Her collage is on her night table.

[Note from social worker]
Athena, It's probably in the back of your mind already, but I spoke to Elizabeth about mounting her butterfly on heavy paper. I have some on the shelf for that purpose. What a wonderful project! —Osa

Sunday, September 18
[Note to social worker]
Osa, Thanks. I've not been feeling well and I told the administrator today that I'm going to take an unpaid leave. Would you care to do something yourself with the two collages?
—Athena

Sunday, September 25
[Note to social worker]
Osa, I'm still on leave but I wanted to drop in today to say hello to Elizabeth. What happened to Margaret and Elizabeth's collages? —Athena

[Note from social worker]
Athena, We have posted the collages on the residents' bulletin board. Go see how great they look. We have discussed ways in which residents can be responsible for keeping the nursing home beautiful and they will be choosing library

prints for the walls. Their own works would be even better but there is isn't much to choose from. —Osa

Sunday, October 9

Today I brought Elizabeth the buttons she made several months ago. I went to the kiln woman and picked up a candy dish and a small vase that were there waiting for me. They were made by Margaret. They are in her room. I've asked her not to part with them until I get them photographed, which is what I did with all the ceramics made by the residents last year and which they gave away as Christmas presents.

Elizabeth's buttons are not successful. The holes closed up in the firing process.

But maybe she can use them in a collage, as she suggested.

[Note to social worker]
Osa, I am so pleased with the way the collages look. I dropped in today just for a visit. I will resume work, however, next Sunday. I'll be in then for two hours.

I would love to have a bulletin board of the photographs of their work last year, hanging in the nursing home. It hangs in my kitchen at the moment.

So I'll be back on a work schedule starting next Sunday. Did I tell you that I have been transferred from the Williamsburg to the Northampton Council on Aging? I do not do any art work with them and I don't want to. It is too exhausting. I like concentrating my efforts and working here in this nursing home.

At the Northampton Council I work part time five days

a week from 9 to 1. Occasionally I will make time to drop over here in the afternoon—on a volunteer and unpaid basis. But I'll continue working here on Sundays as part of the paid staff.   —*Athena*

Sunday, October 16

Worked with Elizabeth. She wrote three letters: to the Daughters of Isabela, to her lawyer, and (in shorthand) to Betty Waller.

Elizabeth started a daisy in beans and wool. Half finished.

Sunday, October 23

Elizabeth and I are continuing with the collages. We are doing a series of them and then we'll decide how they are to be mounted on a single large sheet.

The collage Elizabeth did today is an incomplete bird. Also, I wrote letters with Elizabeth, one to her lawyer about her cemetery plot and marker.

Sunday, October 30

Gertrude still maintains that she doesn't want to get involved, but she has her ears pricked up and she comments to me about Elizabeth's work. For example, "Do you think that bird's beak is long enough?"

Visited with Mary and Lillian for a bit.

Very pleasant afternoon.

Saturday, November 5

Visited with Lillian and Mary; also with Ron and Colette. Worked with Elizabeth. Attended to her correspondence.

Tuesday, November 8

[Note from social worker]

Athena, I certainly think it's interesting that Elizabeth is planning for her cemetery plot. I'm so relieved that you have the kind of relationship with her that she does this kind of processing with you. She wouldn't do it with any other staff member as far as I know.

Gertrude very carefully stays removed from everything—she doesn't get disappointed or hurt that way. She is always curious to know everything but does not want to be involved.

What's your interaction with Ron?   *—Osa*

Saturday, November 12

[Note to social worker]

Osa, I offered Gertrude my arm and she took it, and together we examined the bulletin board outside of the office where perhaps we can mount a collage some time. Gertrude was giving me her opinion, and I jokingly said, "Be careful now. You don't want to get involved."

As for my relationship with Ron, I am going very slowly. If he is in his room, I never disturb him. But if he's in the TV room, I sit down next to him after we shake hands and talk a little about his daughter, whom I've met; about the ashtray he made; about his memory, which he says he would like to improve. Then I take leave. It is very friendly.

Osa, it is such a pleasure to be able to talk to you about the things that are very close to me.   *—Athena*

Worked with Elizabeth on her collage.

Chatted with Margaret, Lillian, and Gertrude.

Colette was very unpleasant towards an unfortunate neighbor of hers in the TV room whose nose was dripping. Some notes so I don't forget. I spoke to Lorraine today about the mall and she expressed a desire to have me take her there on a trip some time.

Also, with Elizabeth I must remember to:
- ✓ continue collage
- ✓ write to her lawyer again re marker on her grave
- ✓ design something special in addition to her name on the stone grave marker (something in shorthand?)
- ✓ borrow book from Forbes Library that Betty Waller recommended
- ✓ write for third time to Daughters of Isabela—either I or Elizabeth.

Saturday, November 19
Elizabeth dictated three letters: one commiserating on the death of a friend; another about membership in the Daughters of Isabela; a third in reference to her grave marker.

Thursday, Thanksgiving
What a nice Thanksgiving. Socialized, which is such a slim word for the effort to make real connections. I visited with everybody whom I know by name and a few strangers. Must do this more often.

Sunday, December 4
Elizabeth did a lot today. Exercised her fingers with a Magic Etch Screen. Then she wrote a letter in shorthand to Betty Waller.

She discussed her gravestone, and that matter now seems settled.

Didn't get to see Ron today.

Saturday, December 10
I am absolutely heartbroken about Mary. She is dead! I can hardly believe it. She was in her forties. What happened?
Spoke to Lillian and she is in a state of shock. She was mumbling about how terrible it all is and how fortunate that Mary will no longer have to suffer.
Had an intense day here. Haircutting was going on. Spoke to Ron, who is friendly to me. Said he hates to get a haircut, but said it with a big smile. Says he gets the works—eyebrows, hair in ears and nostrils, head—everything cut! He looked very clipped.
Spent time with Margaret. We walked down the hall arm-in-arm. She said nothing, not even about her roommate Mary having died.
Eva wanted to know her birthday. I found out it was October second. Apparently she is testing people. Asks everybody if they know her birthday and then corrects them if they happen to make up a date.

[Note from social worker]
Athena, I'm really worried about Lillian. She looks like a worn-out rug! She doesn't mention Mary any longer. I don't know whether she doesn't want to or feels she shouldn't.
Colette has been in better spirits lately. I wish she weren't so mean to our confused residents. Spirits in general seem to be picking up around here. I dread what may happen after New Year's and celebrations are at an end. Eva bowled from her chair today.
Lorraine loves singing and has a surprisingly strong and even

voice. I hadn't heard her sing before.
That Magic Etch Screen is such a fine idea. Maybe others
would also enjoy it. —Osa

Saturday, December 17
I spent some time with Lillian. We talked about Mary. Lillian was too tired to walk with me.
Walked with Margaret and played a game with her in the dining room. I also played with Ron, and then Margaret and Ron played tic-tac-toe with each other.
Ron and I had a long talk about the USS Lang, the destroyer on which he was a gunner during World War II. He told me the different jobs involved in firing a gun. His job was loading the guns.
Visited with Colette, who was cranky.
Visited with Elizabeth. Seemed like today was the kind of day where it did people good to talk. We discussed another one of Joseph Lincoln's books she is reading, and I read some of it to her.
These holidays must be as nerve-racking for the residents as they are for everybody else.

Saturday, December 24
Elizabeth received a fair number of Christmas presents. She dictated a long letter to Betty Waller.

Saturday, December 31
Lillian seemed unreachable today. I fear she is reaching the end. Just my intuition.
Elizabeth, on the other hand, was vigorous today. She asked me questions—very personal (and I was pleased) about myself;

about my previous marriage and what it felt like to be divorced.

Read part of *Wake Up and Live* to Elizabeth.

Elizabeth is still concerned about having enough money to pay for her burial lot and stone. She asked me to check to make sure she has enough money to cover those bills.

THIRD YEAR

Saturday, January 7

I wrote to the U.S. Navy c/o Congressman Silvio Conte, asking about Ron's destroyer. I bet I'll get an answer.

Dear Congressman Conte:

I don't know how to get the enclosed letter into the right hands. I feel sure someone on your imaginative and energetic staff must know.

Thanks from a most appreciative constituent.

Good health to you and best regards.

Yours sincerely,
Athena Warren

(enclosure)

U.S. Navy

Can someone help me?

I have a patient in a nursing home who talks about having been on the USS Lang DD399 during World War II fighting against the Japanese. He, Mr. Ron _____, wants to know what has happened to that destroyer and to the commander whose name he remembers as being pronounced "moosgrubber." (It doesn't seem a likely name, does it?)

You can imagine what a breakthrough this is, having an otherwise silent patient begin to talk about himself.

Sincerely yours,
Athena Warren

Sunday, January 15

I dropped in to tell Elizabeth that I have to cancel our

meeting today. (I was reluctant to send a message on the telephone. Not that it wouldn't be delivered, but I wanted to see Elizabeth's reaction, and if she was *very* disappointed I would have made special arrangements for later today.) But I'll be in tomorrow, Monday, about noon for my session with Elizabeth

Monday, January 16

Ron is telling me some stories about the destroyer he lived on for five years during the war. Perhaps we'll get to write them down.

Elizabeth and I today talked about the "Will to Fail," a concept we've been toying with for a while and which is described in a book that we are reading called *Wake Up and Live* by D. Brande.

Saturday, January 21

Am going to Philadelphia the day after tomorrow. My daughter's baby is due Wednesday. I'll be gone for two weeks.

Had an interesting session with Elizabeth. I think the shorthand interest is petering out.

But she needs to use her brain, and I brought in a kind of crossword puzzle called "Search-a-Word." I'm not good at puzzles but this one is quite stimulating, I find.

Spoke to Ron about the restrictions placed on him as to his possession or use of matches. He said he has no recollection of such restrictions (oh dear....).

Lillian is very upset at being restrained "just because I fell once." She said there are "strict orders from the charge nurse" that she not be allowed to get out of her chair.

Can anything be done?

She doesn't want to upset the apple cart but she also feels very humiliated and resentful.

I'll be dropping notes to several residents to let them know whether I have a granddaughter or a grandson.

[Note from social worker]
Athena, We are looking forward to your return—we depend on you for giving some wonderful individual attention around here. I just feel relieved when I read your notes and know the time you give the residents.   *—Osa*

Saturday, February 25
[Note to social worker]
Osa, I'm so glad to be back. (I had the flu last Saturday.)
I have lots of stuff for Ron about the destroyer that he was on in World War II. I am doling it out.
He was so moved by the fact of a navy officer paying attention to him. He wiped away two tears.   *—Athena*

I went to see the psychiatrist yesterday, thinking I might be out of my depth with Ron. I don't know what memories I might be stirring. The doctor thought Ron would recall only what he wanted to.

My daughter had a girl, 9 lb., 1 oz., Rebekah. I am very happy.

Thursday, March 2
Spoke to the administrator about a change in schedule. Will be working with Elizabeth on Thursdays again for an hour (or so) in the afternoon.

And on Saturdays with Ron. The nursing home will provide the money for the balsa wood for us to make a model of his destroyer (USS Lang D399).

Worked with Elizabeth today. I gave her a shorthand dictionary. She was so pleased.

[Note to social worker]
Osa, Elizabeth wrote the following letter in shorthand to Betty Waller. (She said I could show it to you.)

> Dear Mrs. Waller:
> I recently obtained a copy of a dictionary of Gregg shorthand. I find it very interesting. It contains 26,089 words.
> The plant that you gave me in December is doing very well. It gives me great pleasure.
> Mrs. Warren was out of town for about a month and I am glad to resume the correspondence. And I hope that you are, too.
>
> Sincerely,
> Elizabeth

Osa, I guess it seemed like a "month" to Elizabeth.

—Athena

Saturday, March 4

[Note to activities director]
Joan, Sorry I missed you. Will see you Thursday when I will work with Elizabeth. I'll work with Ron on Saturdays.

Unemotional response today from Ron when we reviewed last week's letter from the admiral. As though it was too much to digest. I left some other material with him today to

read on his own—on the history of the destroyer called LANG.
Maybe he'll talk to you about the ship.   *—Athena*

Monday, March 6
[Note from social worker]
Athena, I didn't get to Ron today. If you can get him to read
it would be a miracle—there is an enormous inertia in him.
He was in really good shape a couple of hours prior to your
coming the last two times. I wonder if he knew you were
coming?   *—Osa*

Thursday, March 9
Today with Elizabeth. We got on the subject of religion.
She taught me a couple of prayers.

Saturday, March 11
Ron reviewed some of his war experiences with me on the USS
Lang as I read from a text (*History of Ships Named Lang*)
describing the ship's movements. This was all part of the large
packet sent by the admiral to Congressman Conte and from
Conte to me.

We'll pick up where we left off. I copied a couple of pictures
of signal flags and Ron identified them.

He said, and I feel he did too, that he enjoyed himself.
[Note from social worker]
Athena, How wonderful that Ron said he enjoyed himself!
It's probable that Ron won't ever remember when you are
coming. He also has a need to protect himself from becom-
ing too attached to you—another good reason for not
remembering when you will come in.

What would you think of working out a schedule of X number of weeks that you will see him with some activities outlined? Having schedule on the wall. This will to an extent define your relationship with him and at the end of the period you can review with him whether to sign up another work period—give him some responsibility for continuing. Do whatever you are comfortable doing. I'm looking forward to hearing from you.   *—Osa*

Thursday, March 16

[Note to social worker]
Osa, Very good suggestion. A calendar is a good idea.
                                                   —Athena

Worked with Elizabeth today. We're reading *Don Quixote.*

Saturday, March 18
Stopped in to see Elizabeth. She was reading *Don Quixote* on her own. I went from one room to another. Annie held my hand. I couldn't understand what she was saying.

Lillian asked me to read a letter to her she received today. I promised I'd help her answer it next week.

Wrote to Margaret on a pad, "Some day we are going to make some more pretty *clay* buttons, okay? Do you remember ever making any?"

She answered "Yes!" in writing.

Session with Ron—very agreeable. Read a couple more pages of history about his destroyer Lang. I made notations on the typed sheets.

In reading *History of Ships Named Lang,* on page 4, paragraph 4, it says that the Lang departed Greenrock on 18 May 1942. Now May 18 is my birthday, and I like to make personal connections with Ron. So I said, "Mmmm, on my birthday. And a week after your birthday."

The paragraph continues, "Following hurried departure, she was put to sea 5 June 1942." It was Ron's turn apparently, and he said, "Two weeks after I was married."

Imagine how pleased I was to hear him make such a personal reference. I did not follow it up because I don't know where I'm going. Especially if what I have heard is really true— that he was an alcoholic who threw his wife down the cellar stairs to her death, presumably after which he lost all memory.

I had given him a present of a mug with ship signals (flags) on it. They will keep it in the kitchen and serve him his coffee in it. Later we'll use those symbols for memory-stirring purposes.

Such a good and satisfying afternoon.

Thursday, March 23
I went to Forbes Library for Elizabeth. She wanted something by Joseph C. Lincoln. Borrowed two books for her with no time limit. Read from one of them to her today.

Saturday, March 25
Lillian asleep, so no letter writing.

Colette cried. Says she feels trembly inside, but is afraid they won't let her out on Easter if they knew, so hasn't said anything.

Ron feels he has a tumor in his head which he thinks accounts for his poor memory. Read more of the Lang's history to him. He concentrated for over an hour before he went out for a cigarette. Wants us to continue reading.

Said he would like to work in a vegetable garden. Loves

tomatoes.

Thursday, March 30
[Note from social worker]
Athena, You may have read Lillian's obituary in the paper. I miss her—but am glad there is an end to her suffering.
I find it incredible that Ron concentrated a full hour on reading!
We will see about a garden this spring. Even just a small tomato patch would be lovely.
Keep trucking!   —Osa

[Note to social worker]
Osa, No! I did not know about Lillian. I'm so sorry.
                                                        —Athena

Worked with Elizabeth. Read parts of *Don Quixote* aloud to her. It's her idea to continue even though she found it tiresome or perhaps tiring to read the book to herself.

Friday, March 31
Am leaving for Philadelphia tomorrow so I planned to work with Ron today. When I came, he was engrossed in a TV dance show and I left him there undisturbed.

Walked around with Lorraine. Why does she tremble so?

Ron is still interested in the destroyer Lang. When I went back to be with him, he read from his *Lang* book aloud. I wondered if he understood what he read.

His hand sometimes trembled as he held the pages.

What a lot of noise. Vacuuming went on right underfoot as Ron read. He ignored the noise. I could not hear him. I suppose

I could say something to the cleaner sometime.

He read two pages and finished the text. Then I said I would ask him next time to start reading aloud again, from the beginning, the *History of Ships Named Lang,* partly for the pleasure of repetition and partly as a way to stimulate his memory by recognition.

I asked him if he gets to drink out of the mug with the signal flags that I gave him, and he said he didn't remember. I asked the kitchen staff and they say he always gets his mug. So I've dropped the subject. Would be nice if he enjoyed using it.

I asked him if he ever put his teeth in, and said that if he did not use them his gums would shrink. He said they make him nervous.

Monday, April 3
[Note from social worker]
Athena, I still marvel at Ron's reading! He has never received this kind of attention here before. I feel less guilty about him knowing you are taking care of him.

Have you set up a calendar with him?

—Osa

Thursday, April 6
Worked with Elizabeth. She wrote a letter in shorthand to Betty Waller.

I was willing to drive Ruth home to visit her ailing husband, but when the nurse phoned to tell him that that was what Ruth wanted to do, he had an absolute fit. He did *not* want to see her.

What a humiliating position for her to be in. The husband sounds mean to me. Must have made life miserable for her. But perhaps she did for him, too.

[Note to social worker]
Osa, No, I haven't made a calendar yet. Would Joan like to? I
don't know when we'll get to it.   —*Athena*

Saturday, April 8

Ron and I made clay buttons. I'll take them to be fired. If they survive the process, I'll ask him to glaze them.

Today he again expressed a desire for fresh tomatoes. I spoke to the nursing-home administrator. Ron is going to be able to have a garden of his own. I'll bring in a spade and a hoe, some string and stakes (unless there are some around here) and he can start digging anytime.

Ron wants to grow tomatoes, yellow squash, radishes, and cucumbers.

This is exciting.

Thursday, April 13

With Elizabeth in the large room celebrating the April birthdays. It may seem like a nice idea, and for all I know residents might not object, but to me it seems merely "efficient" to celebrate birthdays by the month in which one was born. Efficiency has no place where there is sentiment. But maybe I don't appreciate the difference between having a dozen birthday parties a year and having maybe 40 personal parties a year. Still, it would be worth a try to see how morale would be affected using the really personal touch.

Saw Ron for a minute. He's still counting on a garden for tomatoes. There is a possibility that Ron could start this Monday.

Monday, April 17

Ron was nervous about being pushed into digging in the

garden. I think that's because there were too many people around.

The gardener gave us some good top soil and was very nice about digging up the grass and saving it for Sonny, the maintenance man, who wants to transplant the larger hunks elsewhere on the lawn.

A staff member showed a surprising lack of tact in talking about Ron *in front of him* as though he didn't exist. He said, "The tools [fork and hoe] can be kept in the activities office where nobody can get hurt—where Ron won't hurt anybody else and where nobody will hurt Ron." I was appalled. I'm sure Ron's feelings were hurt and he must also have been angry. His reaction was "I don't want to work in a garden."

Thursday, April 20
Elizabeth in bed with a lesion under her breast. I asked her if she has seen a doctor. I would worry about cancer.

The nurses were down on me for talking about cancer. I maintained that talking about cancer is not going to give it to her; but it *is* important to see a doctor, I feel.

Saturday, April 22
I think Ron has forgotten his unwillingness to work in the garden when last Monday someone said something about keeping garden tools from him so he wouldn't hurt himself or anybody else. That remark was a shocker to me, a put-down, however inadvertent.

Ron and I walked around the building to look at the patch of garden that was dug up. It was wet looking, but not muddy. If it turns out that this patch is too wet, we'll look for a better patch.

Ron was in the sun room when I greeted him. I also greeted Colette, to whom I mentioned that Ron was going to have a vegetable garden. She said she knew that, and she also knew that it was full of water.

There was nothing to do in his garden since I had not yet acquired manure or mulch.

I was willing to go back to his reading about the USS Lang. We read in his room. He sat on his bed with his long legs hanging down, not touching the floor. I never realized that his bed is so high. I wonder why. It doesn't make it possible for him to sit on it as though it were a couch. He soon took off his shoes and stretched out on his bed. I then read aloud, sitting in the armchair. He concentrated on my reading. I made notes on the USS Lang pages whenever he actually recalled the event about which I was reading.

He seems to recall none of the details of events. He does remember details of things like the size of the ships, the number of crew, the size of guns.

Ron helped me write a letter to the admiral thanking him for the information and what it all means to him. He said:

1. it "brought back good memories";
2. he didn't know the USS Lang was decommissioned;
3. he would like to make a model of the Lang; and
4. does the admiral have any working drawings?

The time passed easily. We shook a firm handshake and I feel Ron is glad to have something to do with me.

Sunday, April 23

Brought over cow manure for Ron's garden. The gardener turned it into the ground. The administration is very cooperative.

Read from Lincoln's *Galusha the Magnificent* to Elizabeth.

Thursday, April 27
Ron planted two lettuce plants in his garden.

We talked today about gardening. He has a pitcher now to water his garden daily. I'll have to check to see if it is possible for him to do it regularly, that is, if he can be reminded.

For the first time spent some time reading his medical reports. Don't know whether his medication also interferes with his memory.

Tuesday, May 2
Dropped in to check on Ron's lettuce in his garden. He had not watered it. But was willing to do so today, when I said, "Let's go out and check on your garden."

He also was willing to dig a large hole which we left as such. I'm going to get some sheep manure and top soil and fill the hole with good stuff. Then we'll plant one tomato plant in that space.

Spoke to the administrator. She doesn't see any carryover energy into Ron's week from the work he does with me. Too bad. Sometimes that sort of observation throws me. Today the weather is so good my spirits are indefatigable. So I'm what you might call *not* discouraged, if not downright optimistic.

Thursday, May 4
Stanley (the man with no legs) and I went out to look at Ron's garden. Stan laughed. He said, "I wish I had my feet. I'd make a real garden."

Reading *Hope for the Flowers* by Trina Paulus to Ron.

Osa is leaving sometime soon.

What a shame that the turn-over in social workers is so high.

Saturday, May 6

Ron willingly went outside with me to chop up the soil and further prepare his garden.

We have two large holes now (I dug the second one) in which to put our tomato plants next week.

Ron needed a cigarette and asked me for a match. I don't carry them but I suggested that he go inside and get a light.

I went on working in the garden. Then I decided to look for him. He was smoking in the dining room.

I had not given him instructions to return outside. Apparently I would have had to. So I learned something: the importance of giving complete instructions, step by step, without patronizing a person.

Once indoors he watched TV and seemed to be engrossed. I asked him if he preferred not to work in the garden any more, and he said he so preferred.

So I took myself across the room and got a refusal from Colette, who did not want to go out with her walker on the grounds to see Ron's garden. I offered to wheel her. She sneered at that offer and refused.

On my way out, I saw Margaret. We went together to look at Ron's garden.

[Note from social worker]

Athena, How do you find all that courage and optimism? I think the garden is a wonderful, concrete project, visible to all residents. If you can carry through with Ron on the garden until it produces, I think there will be a very positive result for residents and staff. It can be very discouraging for staff and residents to have time only for taking basic care of their bodies. We were brought up thinking we would take care of our bodies so we could get on to the next step—work and have fun. Here that purpose is often missing, here you take care of your body so you will be awake for the day shift and that's about all. Thank you for doing what you are doing, Athena. Fondly, Osa

Thursday and Saturday, May 11 and 13
[Note to social worker]
Thanks for the nice words, Osa.
Didn't write notes. Was in a hurry.

—*Athena*

Thursday, May 18
Went to Forbes Library for some books that Elizabeth might like to have read to her. Brought her a selection by Daphne du Maurier.

As for Ron and his garden, rabbits (I suppose) have eaten both small heads of lettuce. We'll plant some more. He watered his tomato plants which were sitting temporarily in their pots in the foyer.

We'll transplant them after June 1.

Ron wished me a happy birthday. Last week was his.

Sunday, May 21
Ron did not want to put glaze on the buttons he made.

Switched to discussion of World War II and the destroyer he was on.

Briefly visited with Elizabeth and with Stanley.

Saturday, May 27

One of Ron's tomato plants is outside and in the ground.

I am beginning to feel the need for a staff of trained whatever I am—"creative-arts therapist" maybe—to continue the relationships that I have developed with half a dozen women residents. As soon as Ron expressed an interest in a garden and as soon as he showed himself so vulnerable on the subject of his war experience, I felt a responsibility to intensify our relationship. This has meant that I have spent less time interacting with my women friends in the nursing home, and that makes me sad.

Thursday, June 1

Spent a half hour with Ron watering his tomato plant, carrying in lumber and fencing that I've bought to make a fence and gate around his garden (to keep it from the rabbits).

He agreed to water his plant if I would phone in and ask a nurse to remind him.

Saturday, June 3

One and a half hours with Ron, talking, reminiscing—both of us, and doing a little garden work.

Sunday, June 4

Planted two lettuce plants within the fence. Ron toted and watered.

Elizabeth has asked me to help write a letter. I'll come in tomorrow, Monday, especially for that purpose.

Monday, June 5

Elizabeth playing bingo. Will come back again tomorrow.

Tuesday, June 6
Came in to take dictation from Elizabeth. She wrote to the cemetery people settling her account for her headstone.

Sunday, June 11
Worked with Ron on a family history.
First we watered his garden. The tomato plant has two flower buds.
The lettuce is still intact—protected by the improvised screen fence.
Am working in three directions with Ron:
1. The garden.
2. Recalling his memory by means of material on USS Lang.
3. Ceramic work. He has made buttons but so far has refused to glaze them.
Today I asked him to draw circles representing his family. Reluctant. Refused and then agreed. I assured him I was not prying; that he can always refuse to answer my questions. Told him that I was once divorced and that I have no desire to open up a closed area of my past; that if the same applies to him, he must protect himself.
Reminded him of how we met—in the sun room two years ago when he agreed to make an ashtray. It was right after he asked me to help him regain his memory. That is what we are working on. And one way is to recapture his childhood, I told him.

Friday, June 16
Worked some more with Ron on a family history.

He does not resent my asking him questions, he said.

Must borrow books from Forbes Library for Ron (mystery—Agatha Christie and Erle Stanley Gardner; adventure—no cowboys; hunting—safari. These and Ernest Hemingway are his preferences).

Ron had three children.

Thursday, June 22
One hour with Elizabeth. Read to her.

Was greeted by Ron with a handshake.

Thursday and Friday, June 29 and 30
Ron watered his garden.

We weeded it also.

I read a chapter to him of Gardner's book. He said he is going to read it himself.

Friday, July 7
Ron's garden doing well. Green tomatoes are greener and larger. Am anxious to see his reaction when he eats his first red tomato.

Read to him for an hour. Gardner's book. He hadn't read any to himself since last week.

He talked rather personally. Told me his wife was 17 when he married her. He was 20.

Read to Elizabeth. She seemed pleased.

Thursday, July 13
Read to Ron up to Chapter 4 in a Gardner mystery. He is very attentive. We read outside in the sun. He doesn't mind having others around.

Wednesday, July 19
Read to Ron. Got here early. Will take Elizabeth out for lunch. She wants to go to a pizza place. The Council on Aging will send their van with a lift when we are ready.
Phoned the pizza place. They can handle a wheelchair, they said.
The administrator said Elizabeth was admitted 13 years ago. This will be the first time she's been out of the building.

Friday, July 28
Elizabeth wrote a letter in shorthand to Betty Waller, her correspondent. Said to me that she'd go to the pizza parlor at the drop of a hat. "Tomorrow?" I said. "Tomorrow!" she said. Transportation arrangements have been made not for tomorrow but for this coming Monday.
Ron's tomatoes turning pink—two of them.
Am reading him the Gardner story. He has an adequate amount of recall of the story. More than I have.

Monday, July 31
Ron picked his first tomatoes. Almost the size of medium oranges.
Asked him if he remembered my name. Did so on third try.
Elizabeth was positively girlish at the prospect of our going out to lunch today.

Friday, August 4
Ron will have two of his own tomatoes for dinner tonight. They've been ripening on his window sill.
A third tomato blew off the vine in today's storm. It too

will ripen on his window sill.

I find him willing to check on his garden with no coaxing from me, just a simple request. Same applies to being read to from his mystery novel. The story is a bore but we plod along. Neither one of us remembers very much from one reading to the next. We laugh about it.

Wanted to work with Elizabeth, but she was watching a movie. So worked longer with Ron.

Monday, August 7
Dropped in today, and again Ron was willing to water his plants.

Saw the administrator, who suggested we wait until next spring to prepare Ron's next garden because underground pipes are going to be set outside and it's not clear where.

Saturday, August 12
Elizabeth and I talked about plans to go out for lunch again. The trip to the pizza parlor was a big success. She wants to go to Ponderosa next time, a restaurant that she has heard about.

Learned a little more about Ron. His wife is related to Velmette, who works in the kitchen. Nobody in her family wants to have anything to do with Ron.

He is friendly still to me, but I keep away from the subject of his family.

Thursday, August 17
Still reading a murder story to Ron. This was his choice. A little creepy: man murders his wife, lots of drinking, and so on.

Today he said he didn't remember having had *any* tomatoes from his plant. I was startled. He said the tomatoes that ripened on his window sill were given to him by a nurse.

Then he hastened to add that he has no memory.

Nurse just called Ron to go into his room where she "would give him a shave." I wonder why he can't shave himself.

Tuesday, August 22

Ron does not feel like working with me, so I left him another book on destroyers to read. He seemed interested.

Lorraine, who was silently and slowly walking down the hall, seemed depressed. But she did not avoid me. We chatted.

Monday, August 28

Ron out of sorts. I did not attempt to disturb him. Left him on his bed. He did not even want to go out and look at his tomatoes.

Elizabeth looked radiant. Waiting for a bath. Eyes alert and face calm. Beautiful conversation. We talked about a blind patient at the nursing home. Elizabeth said she wanted to hear more about the life of a blind woman.

Friday, September 1

Ron willing to check tomato plants; picked a ripe tomato off the ground but did not want it for himself. I gave the tomato to Stanley.

We read from the Gardner book. Neither he nor I remembered some of the earlier stuff; and laughed. It didn't affect the chapter we read.

Elizabeth asked me for the names of the TV and radio station in Springfield. She's interested in the Sunday program called "The Passionate Fathers," and wants to write to them and send a contribution.

Thursday, September 14

Helped Elizabeth with a business letter; she's sending a contribution for a religious service.

Stanley loved his tomato. Would be glad to have another—with olive oil. I'll have to bring some in. Elizabeth would like one, too, with mayonnaise.

Friday, September 15

[Note to activities director]

Kay, I'm tied up on Saturdays for the next few months. Will come in during the week. Nice to be able to get to know you.

—Athena

Brought in tomatoes from my own garden for Stanley and Elizabeth—with dressing. Received okay from the head nurse yesterday.

Ron doesn't remember what happened to his tomatoes from last week. I checked. They are in the kitchen.

Elizabeth has expressed a desire to do another alphabet book. Perhaps the activities director will be interested in participating. Especially since I would be seeing Elizabeth less this time around than I was seeing her two years ago when we worked on the first book.

Sunday, September 17

I brought in string beans from my garden, overgrown but

still good if they're cooked in soup. Those a little older could be used in the blender for patients requiring liquid food. Then there are those beans that need to be dried out. They can be used like any bean.

Ron's last six tomatoes were picked today. They are green and small but he will ripen them on his window sill. He seems dejected to me.

Saw Margaret. She was cheerful.

Friday, September 22

With Ron, Colette, and Stanley. Short visits with each.

Elizabeth and Ruth and I had a long visit. Conversation about children, responsibility, mother/daughter relations.

Elizabeth was glad to get one of the tomatoes I brought from home, a huge, two-pound one cut in half. I went back in the kitchen and Dorothy gave me mayonnaise for her. I also gave a tomato to Colette.

Promised to bring in the last of the chard from my garden; also three cabbages and more tomatoes tomorrow.

Friday, September 29

Ron and I took down the wire and stakes in his garden and tucked them away in the laundry shed outside.

Read to him outdoors. He can't find his sweater. One of the aides directed him to his jacket, but how does one locate anything that is lost? Is the administrator the one to ask?

Am going to Philadelphia for a week.

Thursday, October 19

Read to Ron.

Elizabeth wrote a letter in shorthand to Betty Waller.

State inspector of nursing homes here. Chatted with him. Joan, the activities director, is leaving for another nursing home.

Friday, October 27
Making progress with Ron. He asked me *again* to help him with his memory.

I assured him that what he did not want to remember would remain encapsulated. And that was okay.

Thursday, November 2
Working with Elizabeth. She asked me for a mystery book, which I will borrow from Forbes Library.

Read to Ron.

Thursday, November 9
I brought in tomatoes. Elizabeth's roommate complained. Said Elizabeth had no right to have any tomatoes in her room.

Thursday, November 16
Am very annoyed that I can't play the Talking Book for Elizabeth in her room because the TV goes all day. There must be somewhere we could go.

Monday, November 20
Elizabeth's spirits are better. Talked about keeping things bottled up. Enjoys being able to talk about this with me.

Tuesday, November 21
Left Elizabeth a Catholic Bible. She was in the toilet and I did not want to embarrass her by going in and talking to her.

Ron said it's okay to wake him up in the future when he's ·
stretched out on his bed.

Met Kay, the new activities director. Good luck to her.
There is such a turnover here.

Monday, November 27

Asked Elizabeth to choose a Talking Book.
She gave me back the Catholic Bible. Don't know why.
She asked me to buy Bisodol. Nurses object. She has the runs.
Elizabeth is distressed at my not being able to make the purchase.
I found out today that Stanley died a couple of weeks ago.
I feel sad. Imagine my not knowing. Why did no one tell me?

Thursday, November 30

Borrowed the record "The Cave" for Elizabeth from
Library of Congress. We used Room 9 to hear it. Not entirely
satisfactory, the room being so stuffy.

Thursday, December 7

(I wonder who here remembers Pearl Harbor?)
Elizabeth received a letter from Betty Waller. Elizabeth
found Betty's shorthand difficult to read this time.

Monday, December 18

Arrangements made for Elizabeth to go out with me in
January to eat.
Spoke to Ron about going to the College Art Museum.
He's not sure he wants to go. Wants to eat and sleep and not
move. But he talked pleasantly enough.

Monday, Christmas
Went from room to room—all morning. Not saying Merry Christmas but merely being pleasant.

Thursday, December 28
Saw Elizabeth.

Friday, December 29
Talked with Ron about marriage. He has strong views on this. Thinks people should marry for keeps.

FOURTH YEAR

Tuesday, January 2

Making artificial flowers out of paper with Ron, a few petals only.

Tuesday, January 9

Visited with Ron. We made a beautiful purple artificial flower. He has it on his night table.

Tuesday, January 16

Ron and I read a *Readers Digest* article together. The article was about machismo.

We talked about home life. He was an only child. He said his parents never showed affection either to each other or to him. But he knew they loved him.

Saw Colette. Her disposition is not so perky.

Next week I'll be away in California. My mother there needs visiting, so I'm leaving for a week. Sorry to have to postpone a date Elizabeth and I had for lunch, a date we made in December.

Sunday, January 28

Back on the job. Ten days in California.

Showed Elizabeth her old alphabet book. She is pretty proud of herself.

Spent an hour with Ron. We looked at Elizabeth's book. He said he'd like to see a Xerox machine. (Elizabeth had used the word "Xerox" to illustrate the letter X.)

Wednesday, January 31

Made a third flower with Ron. It was a flop. The glue showed through. Then Ron covered the glue by using a red Magic Marker. Very successful.

Must buy more clay. What we had was thrown out in the process of remodeling the office.

Saturday, February 3

Stopped in to pick up the Roland Elliott story that Ron's roommate, Fred, is interested in reading. I feel that Fred has made several overtures towards establishing contact with me. I will see how I can fit him in.

Monday, February 5

Told Elizabeth about the distressing news of her shorthand correspondent, Betty Waller. Her husband died suddenly in a hospital. We have no details.

Elizabeth will write a letter of condolence to Mrs. Waller today.

Noticed that Ron borrowed a lighter at the desk and volunteered to light the cigarette of an old resident who was looking around for a light. Don't know if he's ever done that before.

Thursday, February 8

Elizabeth wrote her obituary with a certain amount of strain. Does not want to indicate year she was born.

She found it uncomfortable to be dictating about these matters, but of course it was all her idea.

I mentioned a will.

She said her bankbook is in her lawyer's name. Recommended by Social Security, she said. (I have my doubts.) I must remember to ask the social worker to call about this.

Tuesday, February 13

Had a marvelous time with Ron, as Fred looked on. I opened my purse, which looks like a suitcase, and emptied its contents on the table. What a million things to look at and take off from in discussion. Pictures: one of me, 13 years old, with my parents and sister, pictures of all my kids and my grandchild, identification of all sorts, charge account cards, checks, change, notes, addresses, pens, and pencils. I had the feeling that I was doing something stimulating for Fred and Ron. Then I stuffed it all back in my bag.

I must do this again with other patients.

Friday, February 16

Ron encouraged me about my upcoming talk at another nursing home next Thursday on "How residents can help each other." But he thinks it's a difficult subject.

We got onto the subject of death, which he doesn't like to talk about. When I asked him if I should drop the subject, he said no, we could continue. But essentially we had ended that discussion.

Ron said he would be willing to go out for lunch with me; and I offered my husband, too, as company. We might go to Joe's. But I doubt that it will ever happen, to judge by his basic resistance to leaving the nursing home.

Friday, February 23

Came in to find news of Elizabeth; that yesterday she had a 106 degree fever and was taken to the hospital in a coma.

I'll go to see her this afternoon.

Spent one and a half hours with Ron talking about Elizabeth. Then about females.

He said he had two cousins in Florida and two cousins in New York State.

I would like to go into the subject of his family again.

Wednesday, February 28
Picked up Elizabeth's money for her at the desk and took it to her at the hospital. Elizabeth will not be coming back here. Who knows where she will go? It seems heartless that patients can be shuffled around. The nursing home says they can't save her bed. Damn this whole concept of cost effectiveness.

A little time with Ron.

Four hours this week with Elizabeth in the hospital, keeping up her morale.

Tuesday, March 6
Ron is working on his memory again. We're using a tape recorder.

A nurse said that Ron remembers plenty. She said it's his way of copping out so he doesn't have to be responsible to the law. She did not enlarge.

Also worked with Colette today.

Saw Elizabeth in the hospital this morning. She seemed comfortable.

Thursday, March 15
Visited Elizabeth every day these past three weeks. Apparently she is as cooperative in the hospital as she was in the nursing home. She is getting physical therapy and likes it. Physical therapy is an unheard-of luxury at the nursing home.

Isn't that a shame.

Thursday, March 22

Spent about an hour and a half with Ron. Talked about his memory. He thinks he has a brain tumor. He talked about his navy experience. Also about his father who died when he was 12; a slow death.

I played the tapes Ron worked on with me several weeks ago when we used my tape recorder to record our singing and talk. Ron enjoyed listening.

Pauline, a resident, asked me if I come to see just Ron. I said, "No. Would you like me to see you?" And she said yes. I am pleased.

Saturday, March 31

Brought my litte grandchild Rebekah, who gave pleasure to everyone. I placed her on a patient's lap.

Visit consisted of conversation initiated by Fred. Some participation by Ron, who actually was quite taken by the presence of a child.

Lots of inquiries about Rebekah. Hope to get some young children to come with me on a regular basis.

Saturday, April 7

Fred was explaining his experiment to me: he puts food in his mouth; the teeth automatically chew. He wonders at what point there is a signal for the throat to swallow. As he put it, "This opens up a new avenue of investigation." Ate my lunch in his room to keep him company and to not discourage him from eating since he, like me, belongs to the old school that believes it is rude to eat while another person has no food in front of him.

Saturday, April 14

With Ron. I dislodged the weeds in his garden with a shovel, and Ron removed the weeds and shook out the soil. It tired him to use the shovel.

I had asked Ron to *place* the pot that contained the tomato plant in the spot where we would plant it eventually. But he misunderstood and took the plant *out* of the pot. Not a word of reproach from me. Actually, I may have carelessly said that it would be transplanted in the hole and he assumed I meant right away.

So we planted it and called it an experiment. Today is a little early for planting a tomato plant, but we'll see. One is in the ground now and two are in pots outdoors.

I'll phone and ask a nurse to ask Ron to bring in the two pots if it suddenly turns cold.

Saturday, April 21

Ron and I had such a friendly visit. I said I want to see him take advantage of the rehab occupational training given (unfortunately) on the grounds of the state mental hospital. He doubts he will. Says he is okay here.

Someone brought the two tomato plants indoors.

Asked Ron to say hello to Fred for me when he wakes up.

Wednesday, April 25

Short visit with Ron.

First day after the rains. Garden still doing well. Ron examined it.

Tomato plants coming along. The pots have been moved

outdoors. I think this was thoughtful of someone.

Ron said he would like to leave here. To go to Easthampton.

Told me where his wife "lives," using the present tense. It made me quite upset.

Extraordinary day, beginning at a coffee shop where I noticed I didn't have my change purse and a total stranger, a woman social worker, paid for my bagel.

The day continued in a dramatic way to the middle of the afternoon, when Ron said flatly that he wanted to go back to his wife. (He has never acknowledged, as far as I can tell, that his wife is dead.) That shook me.

Saturday, April 28

Sessions with Ron and Fred.

I'm here with little Rebekah.

The activities director has invited me to a party for the patients at Stanley Park on May 6.

Ron and I watered all the tomato plants. Also talked about going to the cannery this summer. We would can small jars of applesauce, one for each resident, all without salt, all without sugar, and all without apples on account of all the special diets. We laughed.

A long visit with Fred. His wife has already divorced him, one of those unfortunate maneuvers forced on people not poor enough to have Medicaid. Ron wonders if that is legal. I wonder if Ron really thinks his wife is still alive and that he runs a risk of being divorced. He seemed very concerned.

Tuesday, May 1

Spent half an hour talking with Jeannette, the nursing home's young hairdresser (who incidentally did my hair— wash, set, blow dry for only $8.00). She is a warm human being devoted to her work with the elderly.

She is also committed to a career of altruism, working in a Catholic setting doing marriage counseling.

Sunday, May 6

Successful party and trip. Stanley Park is restful. The fireworks there were pretty.

Ron conducted himself at the party in his usual dignified, silent, chain-smoking way.

The nurses warned me about Fred's incontinence. That annoyed me. Fred did *not* wet his pants, and he did enjoy the party.

Wednesday, May 9

Pietro, that's the name of the patient who speaks Italian.

My knowing this came about when I greeted him by saying, "Where are your shorts?" (He looks a bit British in the shorts he usually wears.) When he said it was too cold for shorts, my ear heard an accent. I said, "I bet you speak Italian."

His eyes lit up and he said, "It's only language I speak." Of course he speaks an adequate broken English, too.

In Italian I said, "Anche io parlo italiano."

Well, we're off and running. More conversations to come. And, in effect, I will "take him on" in addition to Fred, Ron, and Pauline. Elizabeth will definitely not be returning to this nursing home.

I wish I had volunteers working with me. It's a shame not to have the time to visit with my early friends here like Margaret, Ruth, Colette, and Lorraine.

Friday, May 18

Ron and I admired his garden. Two radish plants doing well. Ron did not want to pick radishes today but he gave me permission to pick two, one for Colette and one for Pauline. Actually, Ron doesn't want to use his false teeth, so the radishes are not for him, he said. The lettuce is doing fine.

Ron and I installed a piece of a broken crutch in the ground to indicate where the tomato plants are going to climb, if the soil ever dries out. On the head of the crutch is a smooth handle on which we are going to put a label: RON'S GARDEN.

Spoke to Ron about working at Riverside Industries. This is different from the rehab program. It's a sheltered workshop. Not interested, he said, even though he is well enough to leave the nursing home for part of every day.

Ron is going to start Monday being responsible for raising and lowering the American flag in front of the nursing home. I wonder whose idea this was.

We did not mention that today was my birthday and last week was his. Last year he remembered.

Thursday, May 24

Gave Ron some leaves of his lettuce that I thinned for him. He lay on his bed. I sat alongside him in a chair.

Conversation. I started by describing patients in another nursing home who have regular meetings to decide ways of improving their lives. I asked if he wanted such an organization here. He said it would be dangerous; the staff wouldn't want it. "It would be like a union," he said. Then we went on to talk about the textile union to which he had belonged for 15 years. He was a machinist in the repair department.

Traveled to other mills.

I repeat to him that I ask him questions not out of curiosity but in an effort to help him regain his memory.

I asked him if he remembered his asking me to help him with his memory, and he laughed, seeing the absurdity of the question. No, he didn't remember.

Then I said, as a joke, "My name is Athena what?" And he snapped out, "Warren." Friendly and laughing note we ended on.

Sunday, May 27

With Pietro. Talked in Italian about his daughter and about his first wife, who was a Tuscan. She studied music (piano) at Yale. And we talked about his house in town with his second wife, a house which he is giving as a wedding present to his daughter's son who'll be married soon.

For more than an hour I read Pietro *Don Camillo,* a book that came from my father's library. Pietro gets a kick out of the apparently irreligious remarks of the priest Don Camillo. Pietro is a lovely man. Smiles a beautiful twinkling smile.

With Ron for about 15 minutes. He noticed that the two potted tomato plants have been brought back into the vestibule.

Did not see Fred.

Wednesday, May 30

Ron picked radishes; gave one to a patient. No more radishes now. Also picked lettuce, which he's going to have for lunch. He and I sang more songs onto the tape that I made especially for him. Lots of laughter.

Fred indisposed.

Thursday, May 31
Today Fred not doing well. The nurses said I could not see him.
Spent one and a half hours with Ron, recording songs on my tape recorder. He sings fairly well, but best of all, willingly. He does remember fire works at Stanley Park. Says he liked them. He won't claim recollection of anything else.
I insist on shaking hands with Pietro, using his useless right hand (the nurse said this was a good idea, as exercise). He gets a pained expression on his face when I take his hand to shake, but he is cooperative.

Saturday, June 2
Spent two and a half hours here today. Read first chapter of Agatha Christie's *Elephants Can Remember* to Ron, and played back recordings of last week.

Saturday, June 9
I like coming on the weekends. Stopped in to get a glass of milk at noon, and wasn't the cook nice? She brought me a chicken dinner. I felt so welcome.
Ron and I read Chapter 2 of *Elephants Can Remember*. Even I was enjoying it.
I asked Ron my name. Now he hasn't seen me in a week. Right off, no hesitation, he said, "Athena Warren." That is progress.
Fred made me very sad. Wants to find another nursing home and has some scheme, like buying a Buick first, which won't be put into effect, of course.

He knows he is doomed. Damn.

Saturday, June 16

I read to Ron up to page 72 in Agatha Christie's mystery. We got onto the subject of memory again. He talked considerably today. Said that a nursing home is as close as death can come.

He would and would not like to work. Afraid to leave this place. To me, it seems that in his own sad way he knows he dare not leave the nursing home for whatever reason. It is his only haven.

Finished (by skipping some) Christie's mystery. Ron enjoys being read to.

I left him outside smoking and went to seek out the cook. When I returned to the building I saw Ron looking for me. He stuck out his hand *(the first time he has initiated a goodbye)* to shake hands and said he was going to rest. Said he had enjoyed himself.

Another small breakthrough: When I had said earlier, "I'm going to go home," he added, "And I'm going to stay here."

Wednesday, June 20

Came in twice today. Early this morning to deliver freshly picked lettuce from my garden from which my husband had thinned the lettuce heads. All the pickings must have amounted to five pounds. At least Ron hefted it at that weight. All cleaned and washed.

Back again to work with Ron. I have brought two books for him, borrowed from Forbes Library. One is a sophisticated children's book à la A.A. Milne, which no grownup has to apologize for reading. It's called *Are You Hungry, Are You*

Cold? by Ludwig Bemelmans. The other is *Run Silent, Run Deep* by Beach and is about a warship. Maybe that will ring a bell.

Good news about Ron. The charge nurse said that yesterday, unasked, he went down to the mailbox to pick up the newspapers. Imagine that. The nurses were stunned. So was the administrator when I told her this morning.

I feel I am getting through to Ron. Last week he commented on the death-like quality of his life here. Now his spirits are improving. He listed his goodies: good food, gets taken care of, and "you visit me every week."

Saturday, June 23

I read to Pietro in Italian for 35 minutes.

Fred referred to the *Death and Dying* book. Said he had such a feeling last week: as he walked down the hall, he felt his bowels moving and thought he was dying.

Ron left his entire meal. Broccoli, chopped meat, potatoes, dessert. Why? Empathy? I made him a sandwich of the ground meat he left over. He ate half of it.

Ron's room is in the center of all the cleaning activity that is going on. Such a noisy vacuum cleaner.

Fred wants to leave the nursing home. He is always very cordial when I see him, contrary to what I hear about him.

Stopped to visit briefly in four rooms.

Saturday, June 30

Some interesting developments.

With Pietro. Brought my granddaughter Rebekah. Pietro walked with us. She held his bum hand.

Pauline joined our group. Turns out she knows how to

massage. Gave me a massage on my arm. I asked her to massage Pietro's bum arm, but first I asked him in Italian if he was willing. She was sure he wouldn't let her. "He only likes pretty girls," she said. Anyway, he let her massage his arm. He would be willing to let her do this every day. She would be happy to.

I spoke to a supervising social worker who agreed with me that it might be a good idea. I asked her if she'd make it "official" by leaving a note for the charge nurse so that Pauline could be expected to massage Pietro's arm and would be treated with respect.

This is very exciting! Like when I learned that Elizabeth knew shorthand.

Ron played catch with Rebekah, rolling a ball towards her.

Annie has her own doll and she wouldn't let it out of her arms for Rebekah to play with. So I put Rebekah on Annie's wheelchair tray and Annie hugged Rebekah *and* her doll.

Thursday, July 5

Brought zucchini (eight pounds), two huge bags of lettuce, string beans (four pounds) all from my own garden at home. Gave them to the cook in the kitchen for the residents.

Short visits with Ron and Fred.

Tuesday, July 10

Here at 7:30 a.m. to deliver 25 pounds of zucchini just picked this morning from my garden and from my friend Eva Lekachman's garden. The residents enjoyed the last batch, I understand.

Back later in the day for an hour.

Ron affable but firm in not wanting to go outdoors to water his three tomato plants.

Fred "can't talk," Ron says, and in fact it seems difficult for him to swallow.

The two men were sitting side by side when I arrived.

Persuaded Ron to sit out front with me. Told him about a bicycle/car accident my son had, just to get a response from him. His eyes opened wide and he gasped.

Saturday, July 14

Ron seems to be getting a cold. Was cheerful enough when we looked at his tomatoes. Did not want to be read to.

Ron wants to know how TV works. His comment: "Isn't it amazing how all that action and color comes through the air!"

I thought if I asked my stepson Peter Warren to give a simplified explanation, Ron and I might turn it into a children's story.

Fred says he fell down the other day and two nurses laughed at him as if to say, "Look at what I found on the floor." That's outrageous.

Fred seems more bent over as I watch him walk to the john.

Thursday, July 19

Seems as though Ron has a full-blown cold now.

His first reaction today was to stay in bed. I picked five small tomatoes from his garden and took them to his room. He ate two. I told him that he has three large green tomatoes on his plants. He seemed pleased.

Today he did not remember my name.

Saturday, July 21

Read limericks to Ron. He likes them.

Hope to bring my granddaughter Rebekah with me again soon. Ron said he'd like to see her.

Monday, July 23

Pietro is depressed. Would like to have speech therapy as he had in another nursing home. His speech was affected by a stroke. I don't understand why this place offers no physical or speech therapy.

Gave Ron half a bar of chocolate, the other half to Pietro.

Pietro invited me to watch the Pope on TV with him.

Ron watched from the far end of the dining room. Glad to see that he is interested in something outside himself.

I found a note from the charge nurse refusing the social worker's suggestion that Pauline massage Pietro's arm. No explanation. This is frustrating, but I feel I am in no position right now to pick up the challenge.

Friday, July 27

Read an article to Fred and Ron in the sun room. An article on the ERA from Savvy Magazine. Found it at my cousin Nina's house in California earlier this year.

Both men listened. Ron thought we already had equal rights for women. "They can vote, can't they?"

Fred seemed to know of the inequities.

Promised one of the young nurses aides to give her a Xeroxed copy of the article. She said they are studying the ERA in summer school. (Lots of high school kids have paying jobs at the nursing home.)

Friday, August 3

Only with Fred today. He is upset about the death of his brother-in-law. Will see Fred again tomorrow.

Saturday, August 4

Read *Death and Dying* with Ron and discussed what we read. He seems very interested in Kübler-Ross' book and in what amounts to anthropology. I could get some folklore for him later on. If we ever finish Kübler-Ross.

I do enjoy meeting with him.

Spent some time with Fred. He cried. Said "they" had no business preventing him from going to his brother-in-law's funeral. I wonder what I could have done to help.

Fred refused to eat his lunch. But when I acted silly and said, "They'd think I was magic if you ate a little," he ate all his dessert. (This is different from saying, "Eat it for me.")

Said he hated hamburger. I went back to the kitchen and got him some kielbasa. Which he ate.

Promised Fred I'd bring him Robert Frost's poems and read his favorites to him.

Thursday, August 9

Told Ron, Fred, and Pietro that I was going on vacation. Visited with them all. I am going to my first Elderhostel. And then to California to visit my mother, who is in the hospital.

Friday, August 31

Back from California two days ago. Away three weeks. My

mother died August 27 in Los Angeles.

Gertrude said that she was sorry and that she herself is 80 (my mother was 81). Colette, on the other hand, said, "She is lucky."

Brought Ron an avocado plant that I grew from a pit. Spoke to Fred, who was eating. He begged me to give him more details about my mother's death. He said he was with his own father when he died.

I keep going. I won't believe she is dead until the funeral back east.

Wednesday, September 5

Dropped in with four and a half pounds of fresh string beans from my garden and 50 pounds of frozen vegetables from last year: parsnips, carrots, beets, beans; also four pans of baked beans left over from a party of ours.

Met the dietician in the kitchen. Don't know how she feels (really) about this intrusion. She gave the nod of okay, however, to the cook.

By chance I had Warden Lawes' book with me on prison life. Ron and I started reading it, with enormous attention on his part. The book had just been returned to me by a social worker friend.

Wednesday, September 12

Read Chapter 2 aloud of Warden Lawes' book. I had the undivided attention of Ron.

Raining hard. We sat on wet chairs in the vestibule. I read aloud. Then we read in Ron's room. The room needed to be cleaned so we were interrupted shortly. We stood in the vestibule (my dress was already wet from the wet chair) and I read standing up.

Ron often explains words to me which are not familiar. He has excellent recall of a vocabulary that must once have been very large.

Saturday, September 15

Had a long session with Ron.

He insists that his memory is nonexistent. This is no way for us to maintain a discussion. Maybe it is futile. I was exasperated. I am losing patience.

I tell him it *doesn't* matter that he has no memory. (What would he divulge, I wonder, if he admitted to a memory?)

I asked him what he wants in future sessions. He said he wants two things: 1) conversation, and 2) to write a book.

I'll come with paper next week and we'll see how he can be persuaded to write. I suggested that we start with writing nonsense, knowing that there is a grain of truth in all nonsense.

Will see if this is a legitimate direction to pursue.

Examined the tomato plants. Eight more green tomatoes.

Monday, September 17

Ron occupied with TV.

Read poetry to Fred. He is always gentle with me although the nurses say he can be abusive. He asked me about my mother's death. I said I would like to show him an unfinished letter, one never mailed, that I wrote about her death. Would he like to see it? Of course he would. The letter was to a professor to whom I felt greatly indebted. I had taken a short course with him on Death and Dying.

Pietro and I again sang our Italian song, "Avanti Popolo,"

this time to his ten-year-old granddaughter, Judy. She was amused at a foreign song being so lively.

Wednesday, September 19

Fred's birthday. Sixty-five. He reminded me that I promised to bring in a letter.

Ron. We're planning to settle matters relating to a burial plot. Who will pay for it? And a stone. A flat stone on the ground with "AVAST HEAVING" under his name and dates. This is entirely his idea. He does not want to be cremated. And he hopes to live another 20 years.

Although Ron is Protestant, he would like a non-denominational cemetery, if possible.

Monday, September 24

Fred said he has gained weight—three pounds.

Colette wants to die. She is tired, not sick. I helped her walk with her walker.

Brought Fred the poems of Robert Frost. Talked to him and Ron in the TV room briefly.

Left the book for Fred on his bed. Will read to him and Ron next week. They both like Frost.

Saturday, September 29

With Ron and Fred.

Brought Ron cigarettes. He was out of them. Showed Fred a copy I made of Elizabeth's ABC book. He wants to start writing an autobiography. I volunteered to type it for him.

Fred wants to know what happens to his Social Security check.

Ron says he is not interested in handling his money.

Pretty terrific session. All personal talk.

Then I read them my unfinished letter to the professor. I tried to skip some parts, but Fred asked that I read it all.

Dear Professor-friend:

I am trying to put down on paper the extraordinary experience I had with my mother dying. And I am also trying to thank you for having given me the confidence to want to *experience* the process of another's death and not shy away from it.

I held my mother's hand in the last three minutes of her life. I was panicky. I knew I was going as far along with her as she could take me. And all the time I was imploring her to "be peaceful. Be peaceful. Be peaceful."

I kissed and squeezed her puffed-up sweating hand—she was in such a burst of sweat—and I looked up at the heart monitor on the wall and saw the long horizonal line increasing, and I forgot to look at her face as she was dying. And then suddenly everything stopped. The line became straight. [Fred interrupted here and said that he hated those machines.]

I regret that my sister was not telephoned in time. We could both have held mother as she died. My sister, who had done so much for mother, should not have been deprived. She arrived 20 minutes later. Why do I feel so bad? It's because I did not want to have those precious moments *all mine.*

We were stunned and then amazed to see her being washed and wrapped. But why was our mother not allowed to stay with us a little longer? It did not occur to us to halt things for a bit. We hardly had time to say goodbye to a mother whose face was relaxed and beautiful, with a body without all those tubes. But they wheeled her away, and we followed her with our eyes.

(One month later, back East)

Last week, on the same day, the 27th, we had the committal service in the cemetery down the road from my house.

My nephew Tom walked over to the hole, kneeled, spontaneously kissed the box of ashes, and gently holding onto the string around it (that made it look like a present), lowered his arm. And when his shoulder was level with the ground, I wondered if he had hit bottom or whether he had to drop the box the rest of the distance. Several of us in the family moved forward to pick up a handful of soil and drop it in the shaft.

Mario, my son, took a shovel to fill the hole and it seemed to me he was shoveling like a laborer. Then Tom tapped him and said to give Tony, my older son, his turn. Tony shoveled with his back to us. I did not know he was crying. But then I did not know that Mario was crying either until our friend Morty told us.

Tony seemed to be shoveling feathers. The shovel went into the soil gently and was turned over into the hole so silently.

Fred was in tears. I left my letter with him.

Wednesday, October 3

Read some of Kübler-Ross to Fred. This seemed to reach a chord in Fred, whose son died of cancer when he was 19 years old. The cancer first appeared at five years.

I feel we must continue talking about his son. It seems that he died about 16 years ago. Fred says his son would now be 26. So who knows how old he was? The addition is not there. But I'd rather not question it.

Wednesday, October 10

Spoke in Italian with Pietro.
Showed Ron my compass.

The activities director reports a breakthrough with Ron, who played a nursing-home type of bowling game and actually kept score. First time.

Ron and I had a session. Talked about "initiative," and he said he *does* turn on the TV. [He must have thought he had no initiative if he took the trouble to defend himself that way.]

With Pietro. I read an Italian short story to him from the *Don Camillo* series.

Saturday, October 13

With Pietro. I dropped in before breakfast because I happened to be downtown, having driven my son to work. Pietro has an excellent appetite. Oatmeal, poached egg, toast, muffin, orange juice, and milk.

We spoke in Italian. About his daughter and her troubles. She has a daughter who is in a Boston hospital.

Pietro hasn't shaved. He says he doesn't feel well in spite of having a good appetite. I said, "Do you want me to read to you?" "No," and then he says, "Do you want to?" So sweet. And so I did. *Don Camillo.*

Pietro wishes his death would come "tutto a un colpo" (all at once).

Fred dictates his autobiography alternately to Jody and Mimi. They are both lovely young women. I believe they are nurses aides.

I reminded them to put dates on his work.

Tuesday, October 16

With Fred. He read aloud to me for a half hour. His voice never wavered. Read Frost's poems.

Ron listened to Fred read. Noncommittal.

Promised to work with Fred on his writing. He wants his typewriter, and his daughter has promised to send it. If he doesn't receive it in two weeks, we'll write her a note.

I suggested to the charge nurse that the patient down the hall who so persistently repeats the same phrase could be distracted by being allowed to fold laundry or paper napkins.

Friday, October 19

Spent an hour with Ron. He insists that he wants to improve his memory.

Talked about fears. He doesn't recognize any in himself. I can believe this, although I suggested that he is afraid of improving his memory. That was an unnecessary remark. (I have been pretty jangled off and on since my mother's committal.) I wonder why I made it. As far as I could tell, there was no reaction to it.

Fred was being punished for wetting himself and was about to be put into pajamas when I arrived.

We can't find all of the autobiographical work he has dictated. Where has it gone? This stuff has to be found. He says his wallet is missing, too.

Monday, October 22

I was reading to Fred and Ron and we were interrupted by a nurse. "Fred, you're all wet. We have to change your pants."

I think that is a shame. What difference would it make to wait ten minutes more? I can imagine the *humiliation* of being treated as a child. Something must be done about this.

Am reading Ron an old article about the Lawrence strike of 1919. He is very interested. It's the one my father led, in

Lawrence, Massachusetts.

Thursday, October 25

Had a very satisfying long session with Ron and Fred. Fred said he couldn't explain to himself why he often "lets go" and wets the floor before getting to the bathroom. Says it is humiliating.

Read Chapter 2 from Kübler-Ross. All three of us are trying to understand what it means "to accept our own death."

Sunday, October 28

I saw Pietro in his room and turned in there. I read him another story in Italian, a charming story about the father of twelve children whose two-year-old becomes ill and who forced everybody at gunpoint to pray for the child. And the child recovered. "Even God was afraid."

Pietro laughed and was alert and did seem to be enjoying himself, as I was.

Wednesday, October 31

For over two hours I read to Ron about Angela Bambace, a union organizer in the ILGWU and my mother's sister. He told me more about his own union activities and his work as a machinist. All of my references to my personal life are my way of continuing a connection with Ron.

Sunday, November 4

Ron expressed an interest in listening to music. Likes country music, hillbilly songs, also band music. Will try to borrow some from Forbes Library.

Will bring Pauline a carrot from our garden next time. She

asked for one. I did not question her as to whether she could chew it. She wants physical therapy.

On page 35 of the Linda Horn and Elma Griese book on nursing homes there is a suggestion for improving nursing homes which goes approximately:

Instead of asking, "What's wrong?" it's well to identify what is good about residing in a nursing home, and what would make it better, or what would be the "ideal" nursing home.

This approach interests Ron.

Sunday, November 11

Asked Pietro to choose between watching a ball game or being read to. He smiled and chose "un racconto" (a story).

Ron said what he needs is a social life.

He does not object to my taking notes, since we both could use an improved memory.

Tuesday, November 13

Visited with Ron. Asked him if he could sew and replace his missing sweater button. He can.

We decided he will make five clay buttons himself. Am getting the material all set up for this. This is the first clay work we have done this year.

Friday, November 16

I promised Ron to show him my notes and pictures from the time I visited Europe some years ago.

Passed Pietro's door and he beckoned to me to come in, directed me to sit down on the edge of his bed, and said, "Let's sing."

So we sang "Avanti Popolo," an anti-fascist song from his

youth. What fun.

Spoke to Polly. She is 91 and looks 20 years younger. Very agreeable. I'd never seen her before.

She had her head bowed into her cupped hand when I walked by her door. I stopped, turned into the room, and asked if I could help.

"No, I'm just feeling sad." I said that often one does feel sad. One thing led to another. She was widowed at 43. Her daughter died at 49. An operation.

Will visit with Polly again.

Saturday, November 17

A blowout with Lisa, the nurses aide who made the mistake of asking Fred in front of people (me, his daughter, his son-in-law) before he was to go out for the afternoon, whether his pants were dry. Very humiliating, and I over-reacted. I met the aide in the hall and took the liberty of raking her over the coals. I wonder how much this set me back in my good relations with the staff. I will have to apologize to her.

Friday, November 23

Changed our mind about making buttons with Ron today because I brought a story about a bog that my son Mario wrote that Ron wanted to hear. It was published in a high school magazine. Will return to buttons after Thanksgiving.

Read the story aloud to Ron and Fred. Fred thought it was excellent, especially for the scary mood that a bog creates.

Ron listened attentively. He said he had never seen a bog.

Ron and I went outside and we carried (with at least five stops) a huge vat of manure I had acquired. We spread it on his garden for next spring. Also started preparation for a second garden at the other corner of the building.

Thursday, Thanksgiving

Arrived at ll:30 for hors d'oeuvres and to be with Ron and Fred.

Read Fred a beautiful Robert Frost poem on an old man's life in winter. The poem was new to both of us. Had dinner with Ron. Fred went home for the afternoon. I assured him that I was not neglecting my family. We'll all have our dinner this evening.

Helped in the kitchen. Washed odds and ends. Great fun!

Monday, December 3

Clay work with Ron. His comment for each of the five buttons he made was that he "couldn't" and then he did.

The kiln lady, Mrs. Wood, is firing clay tomorrow. Am getting the buttons over to her right away.

Friday, December 7

Last week Beverly, the new activities director, told me about having the kindergarten kids visit the elderly here. What a triumph. She and I see eye to eye on this.

Ron remembered December 7, Pearl Harbor Day. Each year I wonder who does. He had no comment.

Tuesday, December ll

Ron put glaze on his buttons. Also, he glazed some of my old buttons from last year.

Very good morning.

Particularly important was that Ron, on request, got a glass of water to dilute the glaze. I left to get something and when I

returned he had started to glaze the buttons *on his own.*
Several times he said, "I can't do this." I ignored the discouragement and asked if he didn't want a cigarette, which he did.
Then he voluntarily picked up the brush and continued to glaze.
Terrific!

Other people I saw today: Pauline, and Fred who wants
Mario's bog story (I promised him a photocopy), and Gertrude,
who sends regards to Elizabeth. The nurses are all interested in
Ron's buttons. Pietro was not up to singing.

There is an undercurrent all around of illness.

Friday, December 14
Colette died yesterday. Lorraine died last night, and still
another patient died this morning. Everybody is stunned.

Flu is rampant. Don't know how many are ill. Don't
know when it started. I pitched in and served juice this afternoon.

Read to Pietro. Two of the three patients who died
roomed on either side of him. He feels "queer." I feel shattered.

I think there should be a way for patients to say goodbye. Sudden death is grossly unfair to have to deal with
without some ritual.

Tuesday, December 18
Flu is rampant. With pneumonia on its heels.
Doctor's order on door: No Visitors.

* * * *

(I can remember thinking
gratefully of Elizabeth,
safe in   another   nursing
home.)

ENDINGS

There are ends and endings. As Dr. Sherwin Nuland observes in his book *How We Die,* one does not always die with ease nor in the way one would choose. Perhaps my friends in the nursing home who died of flu were grateful to have gone *"tutto a un colpo"* (suddenly), as Pietro wanted for himself. My own ending with the nursing home was such that I could turn to what I had long had in mind—forming and training a small *volunteer* group to visit nursing-home residents 52 weeks in the year. I stayed on after the flu swept us off our emotional underpinnings long enough to taper off my connections with residents, and to reassure them that I would return to visit from time to time. I had come to realize that a more independent kind of work was for me.

My connection with Elizabeth did not stop after she was transferred from this nursing home. I regularly visited her in her new placement. (Do you remember how her room in the nursing home could not be saved for her when she went to the hospital because that would not be cost-effective?) Actually, it was partly due to Elizabeth that our group was made welcome and allowed to function at her new nursing home.

Our small group subsequently became a legal entity—a nonprofit [501(c)(3)] volunteer social agency that we called SECOND MILE (from Matthew V:41 about going the extra mile). Our aim has been to train ourselves and others to offer non-medical services to patients in this hospitable non-profit county hospital, now called a long-term care facility. We are still there. Second Mile is now in its thirteenth year, and I'm in my seventy-fourth.

It seems like yesterday that I went to Elizabeth's funeral; to Ron's; to Pietro's; and to many others'. Now, after more than a decade that Elizabeth has been dead, I find that the legacy she left me was a clear view of what we all did together, and the way I happened to express it one day was in my very first poem:

Elizabeth in a Nursing Home*

*In a field of withering wild flowers
the rain drips and is absorbed.
Rain and wind gather momentum
with no regard for their direction.
The ground swells.*

*Peeking unseen
into this room of
patients, they being offered
such unfamiliar sustenance
as clay, pastel chalk, colored pens;
a book, conversation, a visit—they
sometimes refusing, sometimes
accepting—
it all seems like rampant turmoil.*

*But it only seems that way.
It is the turmoil of growth.*

*Then, a revived stem latches on
to a shaft of sunlight and
leaves unfurl.*

---

*Published *In the Desert Sun.* 1994. Purcell, J. J. III, ed., The National Library of Poetry. Owings Mills, MD: Watermark Press, p. 202.

EPILOGUE

We come to the end of a four-year visit in a nursing home. We ourselves, some day, may be asked to live in such a place. What have we learned from the men and women who move through its pages?

This is *their* home that we have visited. It may be the last home they will ever know, and we watch them as they attempt to make it theirs. They welcome visitors, but not intruders; enjoy activities, but not condescension; and appreciate small opportunities for decision-making. Home for them should not simply be, in the words of Robert Frost's beautiful poem, "the place where, when you have to go there, they have to take you in" ("The Death of the Hired Man," 1923). It should also be a place where they can be comfortable with themselves and others.

Visiting people in this context, we see how the familiar ways of their lives must be adapted to the demands of their new home. Failing bodies and intellects increase the difficulty of their task. Hands that have comforted, held and supported others for years are crippled by strokes and arthritis. Feet that have run errands effortlessly for decades can no longer even walk across the room. Minds that have been active and engaged become clouded and confused. Impaired thought and judgment make new challenges difficult. Modern psychology tells us that human beings engage in solving life problems to the very end. We seldom see such living proof of the difficulties involved as is shown in this book.

What can a home do to ease this process? This new residence offers little space for privacy. Living space is shared with strangers from whom there is no escape. Routines are organized, with little attention to individual needs. Meals come when others fix the time, and may not necessarily be appealing. Adults would like to dress and groom themselves but now may have to wait for help. The running of the home is no longer up to those who live there, but the responsibility of those who manage its routine.

Having shared their experience, are we better able to create the home these men and women need? As they speak to us in these pages, we catch small messages, sometimes silently expressed. Some speak of loss of confidence as their abilities wane. Elizabeth, seemingly aloof and hunched in her wheelchair, emerges, with encouragement, into a thoughtful person of some ability. Colette, whose stroke has left her weak and hopeless, yearns for real work and for competence in writing so that she can write to her daughter. Others show us that bright and friendly minds, hidden behind disabilities, are longing for human interaction. Margaret, very deaf, participates in activities with vigor and interest. Lorraine has a sense of humor which can be lost in a busy place. All must make peace with themselves and their mortality. Death is a frequent visitor, but there is little time to reflect on its significance. Some, like Ron, have seemingly lost their capacity for reflection with their loss of memory.

These are the people who saw that we were fed and clothed and comforted when we were small. They kissed our hurts and kept us safe from harm. Now they are strangers, no longer able to fulfill the roles in which we knew them many years ago. What do they need to be in order to be at home?

We see that they need time to reflect, to experiment without a sense of failure. With time, many can reestablish a sense of self, and even of self-worth. It is our turn to listen and to attempt to understand what their changing capacities mean for them.

It helps when they can tell stories of their past, drawing us into their former lives. It also helps when, in creating gifts for family or friends, they can reach back to the community that was their life until now.

They need us to take them seriously, to treat them as the experienced adults they are, to respect their privacy and personal space, and to offer them dignity. Amelia is unhappy and needs to share her feelings with someone who will listen. Elizabeth blossoms with attention, and is able to develop new relationships and self-respect. Mary is pleased that she can teach the author something about mending rugs.

They also need our support as they struggle with some final problems outside of their present narrow world. Elizabeth wants to write a letter to a friend. Later she asks for help in making a will and arranging for a burial plot. Lillian is devastated by Mary's death, but finds it hard to talk about its significance. Ron worries about his memory, but can he face the facts that recalling the past would bring? A letter from an admiral brings back good memories, but are there others he doesn't want to return?

Into the Lives of Others reminds us of how closely we human beings are knit to each other, and of how, through life, we understand life in community with one another. As Harry Stack Sullivan writes in his work on theoretical psychiatry, "Each person. . . is involved as a portion of an interpersonal field rather than as a separate entity, in processes which affect and are affected by the field" (*Collected Works of Harry Stack Sullivan,* Vol. 1, p. xii). In the pages of this Warren's book, we learn the importance of creating community in the nursing home through the therapeutic use of a professional who takes part in the daily routines of residents as a "participant observer." The role cannot happen without deliberate thought because, as Osa, the social worker, writes, "It can be very discouraging for staff and residents to have time only for taking basic care of their bodies." *Into the Lives of Others* gives us important clues as to how this can be done.

—Ruth Carson West, Ed.D.

Acknowledgments

I feel I have succumbed to convention. That's because I had planned to list 79 people on this page, but almost everybody said, "That is idiotic, listing 79 people to whom you acknowledge thanks."

Well, there *are* 79 people, and maybe even more. And it is painful to cut out names.

There are patients—present ones—to whom the story the book tells is of intense interest. There is Jane Hillman, who read the first part of the book and corrected my ceramic terms in the interest of accuracy. There's my immediate family (only two of whom—my husband and my younger son—allowed themselves to be tormented without using expletives) who read a ream of re-written "Introductions" and "Conclusions" (neither name now being retained).

There are my two sisters-in-law, Margaret and Helen. There's my sister Clytia, who has been magnificent; there's my oldest friend (from Manumit), Dr. Beth Trussell; and my first mentor, Elaine Ostroff; my friends the Eric Lampards; my dear friend Mary E. Dimock. There's Bet MacArthur and Ruth Carson West, and the graphic artist Paul Cheda, now director of the Williamsburg Council on Aging in Western Massachusetts. There's Marcia Yudkin and Joe Aloysius Kennedy, and . . . .

But this is grossly unfair. There are so many others. And every little bit that people have contributed has mattered. I shall ask my young grandson, Alec McAlister, to draw a Pooh-type balloon and we'll send it off to catch up with you, my unnamed friends and relatives.

A.M. 1994

A list of the books and other reading materials mentioned in this book can be obtained by writing to the author c/o Second Mile, Inc., Williamsburg, MA 01096.